C000144095

Printed by Book Printing UK www.bookprintinguk.com
Remus House, Coltsfoot Drive, Peterborough, PE2 9BF

Printed in Great Britain

ISBN 978-1-3999-1779-7

Foreword

I left Edinburgh University in 1976 aged 23 with a degree in Social Work and no intention of becoming a social worker. I was in limbo. Within three months, a random opportunity took me to the Sea of Galilee. One thing led to another, and I retired at Christmas 2020 aged 67 having spent my 44 year working life organising pilgrimages.

When I retired, I passed the family business into the capable hands of Rosemary Nutt, my business partner for most of my working life. Rosemary was joined by Paul Ellerby and they successfully guided McCabe Pilgrimages into a new era.

Sadly, Rosemary died, suddenly and unexpectedly, only a year after taking over and shortly after I completed this book. She read and enjoyed it and we reminisced about a hugely fulfilling forty year partnership.

This revised edition is printed in Rosemary's memory with proceeds going to projects supported by The McCabe Educational Trust including Biliki in Georgia, which was close to Rosemary's heart. We are grateful to McCabe Pilgrimages for covering production costs.

Alistair McCabe

February 2022

Rosemary Nutt 1963 - 2022

Contents

Stepping Stones To McCabe Travel

1976 -1982

The First Forty Years

The Early Years   1983 - 1991   21

Our Golden Age   1992 - 2000   63

McCabe Educational Trust   69

Survival   2001 - 2010   119

A Decade of Calm   2011 - 2021   133

Retirement and New Beginnings   159

Stepping Stones

1976 -1982

If anyone had told me at my graduation that I would spend my life working with the church, I would have laughed. I graduated with a career path in social work. My first and only employment as a social worker was in Edinburgh's Grassmarket, then one of the poorest areas of the city with many shelters for the homeless and a big drink and drugs problem. Stuart Lynch, who would become a McCabe Director, also worked here for a time. It was a soul-destroying job requiring real dedication – which I did not have. The team were understaffed and under resourced and the number of cases each worker was supposed to look after was totally unmanageable, so the job was essentially crisis intervention as opposed to regular care of vulnerable people.

It was my father, a Church of Scotland Minister, who drew my attention to an advert in an obscure church publication called *Manse News* for an Assistant Warden to work at the Church of Scotland 'Hospice' in Israel. The requirements listed included hotel management experience and a working knowledge of Hebrew. My father pointed out that the Scottish church was a small community, the magazine was only read by ministers, and it was highly unlikely that many applicants would have these qualifications. He was right. I was the only applicant and, after a couple of interviews, I was offered the job.

A few months after graduating, and twenty three years old, I was living in Tiberias beside the Sea of Galilee. Since my early years in India, I had never travelled abroad or been on a plane. Worse, I couldn't place Israel on a map. My naivety stretched to no knowledge of Palestinians, or the fact that Israel had taken part in the Yom Kippur war three years earlier with the Syrian army almost over-running Tiberias.

Tiberias

This was to be the random decision that would give direction to the rest of my working life. The 'Scottie', as everybody called it, was a much-loved part of Tiberias history. Built around 1900, it was once the only hospital in the area, with grand buildings set on terraces rising from the lakeside. When Israel became an independent country and developed its health service, the hospital became redundant, and was converted into a Guest House for pilgrims visiting the Holy land.

The property I came to in 1976 was in poor condition, with multiple problems. I was fortunate in the appointment of Mary Ohannessian as my immediate boss. Mary had just retired from a lifetime of service in various church institutions in Jerusalem, spoke eight languages, and was enormously capable. We looked at the state of the fabric. Hard to believe, but the beds were mostly the original metal framed hospital beds. We replaced them. We then added private facilities to each bedroom. The kitchen was in a different building to the dining room. We moved it. Air-conditioning was installed in the dining room and lounges. None of this was high quality. Our budget was small, and everything was done ad hoc with little long-term planning. We tried unsuccessfully for a name change. Hospice was a correct term for pilgrim lodgings but was now more associated with end-of-life care, and the title of Warden was more suited to a prison. Why not rename as the Sea of Galilee Centre with a Manager in charge. These changes did come, but long after my time.

Life at the Scottie suited me and looking back was a very special period in my life. Mrs Mary (as she was known) became my mentor, taught me so much, and became a friend for life. We were assisted by five or six volunteers, students on gap years and the like, who gave the place its Scottish character and a vibrant social life. The dozen or so local staff were mostly Jewish immigrants from Morocco and they became like a family to me. In addition to all this, we converted the flat above the church into six self-contained rooms which were rented long-term to United Nations peace-keeping officers. All different nationalities, they would come to breakfast in their uniforms, adding to the cosmopolitan mix. I played rugby for Mevo Hama kibbutz, and got to know a group of dedicated kibbutzniks, my own age, living on the border with Syria, including Lenny from Glasgow who still lives there and we keep in touch. There were three Alistair's in our community: big Al, Irish Al, and Little Al. I was Little Al! My girlfriend Patsy and friend Lorne joined as volunteers and visitors from home were regular.

At this time, Israel was occupying the Sinai Peninsula and we wouldn't think twice about driving 300 miles down to the Red Sea for the weekend. Our favourite spot was Dahav, where we slept in straw huts as part of the Bedouin village. Today Dahab is unrecognisable with multiple deluxe hotels and a large hippie community. Sharm El Sheik only had one small hotel then. Today it is a city.

A Tiberias working day would start with an early morning visit to the vegetable market. I can still name most fruit and vegetables in Hebrew, but my language didn't progress much beyond that. Breakfast at seven, was followed by a morning working in the office or around the property, with lunch around noon. Afternoons were too hot to do much, so this is when we had our main sleep, waking around four to prepare for guests returning from their day. After dinner, we would head for Jose Cohen's Galei Gil café on the waterfront, or Amos Yaskil's gallery bar, run by fellow ex pat James Bigbee. (James would later set up Inner Faith Travel in Australia copying – with our permission - everything we did at McCabe Pilgrimages). We took full advantage of the coolest part of the day and night time sleep would sometimes be just a few short hours. In the summer, the temperature rarely dropped below a hundred, too hot to sleep indoors so we would sleep on the balcony.

We had loyal Israeli guests, who liked the Scottish atmosphere and Christian workers from around the Middle East would come on retreat. I remember nurses visiting from a mission hospital in Gaza and regret not taking the opportunity to visit them, at a time when the border was open. We would host local Christian conferences.

6

Dahav, Gulf of Eilat

7

Arab families would come and stay, and the challenge was often to know exactly how many family members were staying in a room. Most of our guests were pilgrim parties and the biggest provider was Inter Church Travel. In those days, a typical group would number more than forty participants, and it was common for a pilgrim group to stay for a full week. Nowadays, two or three nights in Tiberias would be normal.

Some groups would come and go, with little interaction, but with others we would make firm friends, with guests joining us in the waterfront cafés late into the evening. Unsocial flight times would see us carrying luggage and waving goodbye in the darkness before dawn, and an abiding memory is carrying endless suitcases up and down the many stairs.

Facilities were sparse, but the Scottie had a unique atmosphere ideal for pilgrimage. Large balconies overlooking the lake were ideal for group meetings, and evening socialising. We would set out chairs and an altar on the terraced lawn for communion services as the sun rose over the lake. I do remember once checking before a group service, to find the gardener had a sprinkler spraying all the seats!

We would join pilgrim groups and visit the scene of Jesus ministry. I can remember sending postcards home of Capernaum, Nazareth, Cana, and the Mount of Beatitudes. My father kept them all. As a Minister he had never seen these places – or even dreamed of seeing these places. Few church goers then had been on a Holy Land pilgrimage. I found it a mind-blowing experience to be living and working 'in the parish of Jesus'.

Visiting Jerusalem for the first time is something I will never forget, especially the markets in the Old City. We would stay at St Andrew's Guest House, which could not have been more different from its sister Tiberias property. Here, Miss King presided over a leftover from British rule. General Allenby's portrait dominated the lounge and guests were more likely to be diplomats than pilgrims. The British consulate was in the garden. The St Andrew's year was punctuated by Scottish occasions attended by the international community, and the church congregation were mostly Americans.

The Mt. of the Beatitudes

A belated gap year experience

After Tiberias, Patsy and I planned a three-month trip through Europe, or until the money ran out. Neither of us had travelled before, so it was a big adventure. We sailed from Haifa to Athens then on to the Greek island of Mykonos where we rented a room and would buy retsina, bread, cheese and olives and eat well on our small budget. Taverna meals would be calculated, taking advantage of bread and cheap items like moussaka. We continued to the islands of Samos and Chios and crossed over to Kusadasi in Turkey and travelled by train across Turkey to Bandirma on the Sea of Marmara. We sat in the guard's van and locals shared food with us. An overnight ferry crossing and we arrived in Istanbul, where our money ran out! My father came to the rescue and wired £50 to a local bank. This was just about enough money to get home – by bus.

The 'Magic Bus' plied regularly between London and Kathmandu! We joined from Istanbul to London. The clientele were impecunious young people like ourselves. We changed bus in Athens and drove through Yugoslavia to Venice and on to Calais and London. I still remember the smell of breakfast when we boarded the channel ferry, with absolutely no money to buy anything! The coach from London to Edinburgh felt like a short hop after seven days on European buses.

I wouldn't choose to do a bus trip like this again, but I think our children sometimes miss out by having money. I have spent most of my life travelling, and journeys with funds are less likely to throw up the encounters which make travel exciting. Our journey lasted about six weeks, and I was home in Scotland, unemployed.

Joining Inter Church Travel

'Alistair, I want you to be me in Israel!'. The year was 1978 and I had just returned from Tiberias and, now 25, was an unemployed (some would say unemployable) social worker. Inter Church Travel and Orientours were the big two Holy Land pilgrimage companies, both based in London. ICT was Christian, run by Canon Arthur Payton. Orientours was Jewish, run by Morris Perry. I had got to know the Inter Church staff while working in Tiberias, so wrote to Arthur to see if there were any openings for me. Arthur agreed to a meeting (but without travelling expenses) and Patsy and I took the bus to London, slept on my friend Bill Trimble's floor, and the next morning visited the Pall Mall offices of Inter Church. The quotation above turned out to be my only job description. And so, the McCabe Pilgrimages story began.

I represented Arthur in the Holy Land for almost two years, meeting and greeting groups of pilgrims, befriending hoteliers, guides, and drivers and developing an intimate knowledge of pilgrimage from all angles. And yes, I was a spy, reporting bad practices back to Arthur in London.

I had found the perfect job. I wasn't paid much, but I had very few expenses. I commuted between Jerusalem and Tiberias. In Jerusalem, I rented a room in the same house as a travelling student, Bruce Kinsey, who would be part of the triumvirate that started McCabe, and I also rented a room in the United Nations quarters at the Scottie in Tiberias. In a typical week, I would meet three or four groups arriving at Ben Gurion airport and join them for parts of their programme, checking all arrangements were in order. I had the best of both worlds, with a new social life in Jerusalem based around Bruce and the family we were staying with, and a return to my old haunts in Tiberias. I would typically divide the week between north and south, travelling up and down the Jordan valley with pilgrim parties. I worked hard, played hard and learned the pilgrimage business from all angles. As important, the people in the pilgrimage business got to know me.

Fate took a hand. Geoffrey Pepper, the office manager in London, took ill and I was invited to join the London team. I was offered the job on a Friday and started work in London on the Monday morning. Second time in London, first time in an office, first time in front of a typewriter, staying with family friends and quickly realising London is an expensive place to live. Three years working in central London, in the iconic Thomas Cook building at 125 Pall Mall completed my apprenticeship.

Inter Church Travel with Arthur Payton

I joined an ICT office with a cast of larger-than-life characters brought together by Arthur, who had a history of befriending waifs and strays – like me. Alcohol was a common denominator and, coming from my strict church upbringing, this shocked me. The Honourable Geoffrey, of the Guinness family, would pad around in his socks with a glass of 'orange juice'. Arthur would retire to his club on Pall Mall each day for a three-hour lunch, and sleep at his desk most afternoons. Geoffrey was a depressed former alcoholic publican who would spend hours typing a letter as a cover note to send a brochure. Ursula, who would become McCabe's first employee, had the unenviable task, as Arthur's secretary, of protecting Arthur from visitors! Joining this eclectic mix were Theresa and Don, Thomas Cook employees approaching retirement who had been assigned to ICT rather than move out of London to the new Thomas Cook headquarters in Peterborough.

Don, with forty years' experience in travel, was totally bemused by the set up. I enjoyed joining him in the pub at lunch times, when he would tell stories of the glory days of Cooks. Theresa was aristocratic Polish, a devout Christian and kept an air of aloofness to the chaos surrounding her. I would fight constantly with accountant Malcolm, who saw it as his duty to delay paying any bills for as long as possible. Into this mix came Rosemary Nutt, a student helping in the holidays. Her father was a behind the scenes director and daily lunch companion of Arthur at their club, Brooks's. I found my feet and fitted in, looking after the Holy Land pilgrimage side of the company.

The 'Christianity' of ICT was totally new to me. I didn't really know the term 'evangelical' because my church upbringing was so narrow, that I never really encountered any Christians who were not evangelical. Arthur was a 'High Anglican' and so were many of our tour leaders. A privilege of working in pilgrimage has been exposure to so many branches of the Christian church and their clergy and congregations. Getting to know the church in the Holy Land was an eye opener for me, as it is for many new pilgrims. Visiting the Church of the Holy Sepulchre for the first time, containing both the Hill of Calvary and the Tomb of Christ, was confusing enough, but to find the Greek Orthodox, Egyptian Coptic, Armenian and Roman Catholics all competing for space, prestige, and influence– not to mention the Ethiopian Christians living on the roof – was a revelation to me and to many first-time pilgrims.

A big part of my work at McCabe has been to help people see past alien and confusing forms of Christian liturgy to appreciate the reality of where they are visiting.

I paint a bleak picture of Inter Church Travel but, for most of its life, it had been a company with purpose led by a man of vision. Arthur had started out as a hard-working priest in Toxteth, a challenging area of Liverpool, where he developed a passion for church unity. When he founded Inter Church in the 1950s, his ambition was to help re-unite the Roman Catholic, Anglican, and Orthodox churches and he saw pilgrimage as a great medium towards this goal.

An early initiative was a series of 'Cruises of a Lifetime' where he would charter a ship and feature visits to the great church centres around the Mediterranean. On board would be high ranking British church leaders and official visits would be arranged with the Pope in Rome, the Ecumenical Patriarch in Istanbul, and the Coptic leadership in Alexandria. A highlight would be the visits to Jerusalem and Galilee. Arthur was an amusing and eloquent speaker with an ebullient personality and led from the front, but he was always churchman first and businessman second.

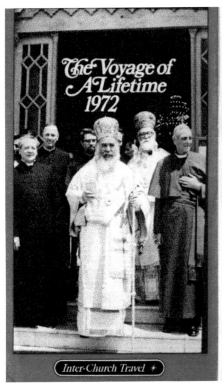

The S.S. Fiesta of Chandris Cruises

Voyage of a Lifetime

Ten years ago saw the first Inter-Church Travel "Voyage of a Lifetime"—this annual cruise—and there is only ONE—has proved itself year after year to be a tremendous success as a holiday packed full of interest and excitement. 1972 will be no exception!!

The "Fiesta" of Chandris Cruises is a small but luxurious vessel—the itinerary is what the doctor ordered!!—sightseeing at most unusual places on the way to the Holy Land—then five days visiting the peaceful shores of the sea of Galilee and the City of Peace—Jerusalem and Bethlehem.

Staying in excellent hotels in Jerusalem for four nights, passengers travel each day in comfortable coaches accompanied by clergy chosen for their intimate knowledge of the Biblical sites you will visit.

After all this there are nearly four days at sea on the return to Venice—time to relax and enjoy "ship's fun and games"— discussions—worship or just rest—truly the finest 'Package' of holidays all in one. Book now—limited space!

Published by Inter-Church Travel Ltd., 125 Pall Mall, London SW1 5EN. Tel: 01-930 2241 (Inter-Church Travel Ltd. is a wholly-owned subsidiary of Thos. Cook & Son Ltd.)

I arrived in the company shortly after Arthur's vision collapsed.
A chartered cruise ship ran aground before picking up its passengers, and a substitute ship had to be chartered at short notice. There was no insurance for this eventuality and Arthur had to pay for both ships. The money was not there. Thomas Cook stepped in and bought the company for ten pence, plus the debts. Arthur did a personal deal that he would remain in charge until his retirement in a few years' time.
I joined a company run by an MD who had lost interest and a Thomas Cook hierarchy whose hands were tied until Arthur left.

Inter Church being a bit of a rudderless ship gave me opportunities beyond my experience. Most memorable was our first group from Nigeria. The pilgrimage was planned at short notice for a party of fifty from Lagos - no email or mobile phones and all arrangements made by correspondence. The party would make their own way to Tel Aviv, where I would meet them together with Arthur Smith, Archdeacon of Lincoln, who was going to be their Spiritual Leader. The arrangement was for them to pay us on arrival. They did not arrive. We discovered they were stranded in Rome without the necessary visas to visit Israel.

I flew from Tel Aviv to Rome, and still remember this first visit to Italy. I learnt that first experiences are very special, and always felt that responsibility as a tour operator taking people somewhere for the first time. I had a job to do, but I also explored Rome to the full.
My favourite building is the Pantheon. With origins as a Roman Temple dating back to the time of Christ, the Pantheon looks like it was built yesterday but has been in continuous use for a thousand years, currently as a Roman Catholic Basilica. Another highlight was seeing the opera Aida performed in the open-air setting of the Caracalla baths.

But I was in Rome for a reason. I contacted the Israeli embassy who co-operated, but it took a few days for visas to be issued, and I used this time to walk every inch of this great city. A first experience I have never forgotten.

Payment was the next issue. In a memorable evening, I collected payment in cash, in lots of different currencies. EL AL flights were re-arranged, and we arrived in Israel a week late. We would arrange many Nigerian pilgrimages, but this was the first and we didn't know what to expect, or what the party expected of us. Arthur Smith was, I think, a little apprehensive and the group was bemused by this very English clergyman. For me, it was simply a fantastic experience.

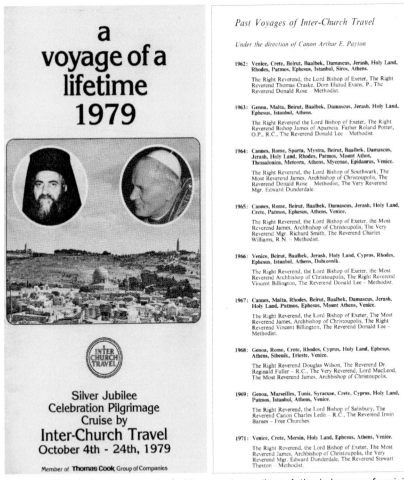

a
voyage of a
lifetime
1979

Silver Jubilee
Celebration Pilgrimage
Cruise by
Inter-Church Travel
October 4th - 24th, 1979

Member of **Thomas Cook** Group of Companies

Past Voyages of Inter-Church Travel

Under the direction of Canon Arthur E. Payton

1962: Venice, Crete, Beirut, Baalbek, Damascus, Jerash, Holy Land, Rhodes, Patmos, Ephesus, Istanbul, Siros, Athens.

The Right Reverend, the Lord Bishop of Exeter, The Right Reverend Thomas Craske, Dom Illutud Evans, P., The Reverend Donald Rose Methodist.

1963: Genoa, Malta, Beirut, Baalbek, Damascus, Jerash, Holy Land, Ephesus, Istanbul, Athens.

The Right Reverend the Lord Bishop of Exeter, The Right Reverend Bishop James of Apameia Father Roland Potter, O.P., R.C., The Reverend Donald Lee - Methodist.

1964: Cannes, Rome, Sparta, Mystra, Beirut, Baalbek, Damascus, Jerash, Holy Land, Rhodes, Patmos, Mount Athos, Thessalonica, Meteora, Athens, Mycenae, Epidaurus, Venice.

The Right Reverend, the Lord Bishop of Southwark, The Most Reverend James, Archbishop of Christoupolis, The Reverend Donald Rose Methodist, The Very Reverend Mgr. Edward Dunderdale.

1965: Cannes, Rome, Beirut, Baalbek, Damascus, Jerash, Holy Land, Crete, Patmos, Athens, Venice.

The Right Reverend, the Lord Bishop of Exeter, the Most Reverend James, Archbishop of Christoupolis, The Very Reverend Mgr. Richard Smith, The Reverend Charles Williams, R.N. - Methodist.

1966: Venice, Beirut, Baalbek, Jerash, Holy Land, Cyprus, Rhodes, Ephesus, Istanbul, Athens, Dubrovnik.

The Right Reverend, the Lord Bishop of Exeter, the Most Reverend Archbishop of Christoupolis, The Right Reverend Vincent Billington, The Reverend Donald Lee - Methodist.

1967: Cannes, Malta, Rhodes, Beirut, Baalbek, Damascus, Jerash, Holy Land, Patmos, Ephesus, Mount Athens, Venice.

The Right Reverend, the Lord Bishop of Exeter, The Most Reverend James, Archbishop of Christoupolis, The Right Reverend Vincent Billington, The Reverend Donald Lee – Methodist.

1968: Genoa, Rome, Crete, Rhodes, Cyprus, Holy Land, Ephesus, Athens, Sibenik, Trieste, Venice.

The Right Reverend Douglas Wilson, The Reverend Dr. Reginald Fuller – R.C., The Very Reverend, Lord MacLeod, The Most Reverend James, Archbishop of Christoupolis.

1969: Genoa, Marseilles, Tunis, Syracuse, Crete, Cyprus, Holy Land, Patmos, Istanbul, Athens, Venice.

The Right Reverend, the Lord Bishop of Salisbury, The Reverend Canon Charles Ledit – R.C., The Reverend Irwin Barnes – Free Churches.

1971: Venice, Crete, Mersin, Holy Land, Ephesus, Athens, Venice.

The Right Reverend, the Lord Bishop of Exeter, The Most Reverend James, Archbishop of Christoupolis, the Very Reverend Mgr. Edward Dunderdale, The Reverend Stewart Thexton – Methodist.

One ambition that never came to fruition was to continue Arthur's legacy of cruising. Perhaps mindful of the risks involved and Arthur's eventual undoing.

Inter Church Travel after Arthur Payton

Arthur retired in 1981 and Thomas Cook came in with a fresh broom. We moved to new offices off Regent Street, and most of the old staff retired. Cooks appointed a professional MD to run the company; in fact, they appointed two. Revd Peter Mallet had recently retired as Army Chaplain General and was appointed as a figurehead to maintain church connections. Douglas Cady was appointed MD. I remember meeting Doug for the first time, sitting behind his desk smoking a cigar. He knew I had applied for his job, and I don't think he really knew what to make of me. I did my job and would often accompany Doug for long liquid lunches. I didn't appreciate it at the time, but the power in the office had swung to me. Peter and Doug had not yet visited the Holy Land and neither had any background in pilgrimage. I became the 'fount of all knowledge' which I didn't mind. It became clear that Doug didn't have much empathy with pilgrimage or with our regular clients and I increasingly felt trapped in my junior position.

For me personally, the move to London had been difficult on many levels. Number one was financial. My first ICT salary was around £5,000 – an increase on what I was paid in Israel, but there I had very few expenses. In London, after I paid my rent and travel costs into the city centre, and bought food, there was little left to enjoy life. I can remember living in a one-bedroom flat in Sutton with the unforgettable address, Sherwood Court, Robin Hood Lane. I lived on my own for a year and have memories of going home some weekends and not speaking to anybody from Friday night to Monday morning and having absolutely no money to do anything. Two lonely years in London ended with a chance meeting with Steve, who had a room available in a flat in Earlsfield. When Arthur retired, I had just moved there and, for the first time since coming to London, felt secure and at home, more so when Lorne, who had shared my Scottie experience in Israel, moved in. Rosemary needed somewhere to stay and, for a while, also became a flat mate.

The decision to leave Inter Church was not easy with finance being the biggest worry. I had no savings and little left over at the end of each month. My parents were proud of what I was doing and the relationships I was building with eminent church people and worried that I was taking a step too far. I had a career ahead of me in Thomas Cook, the biggest name in travel, and I was going to give this up and step in to the unknown. Renting an office and hiring staff would not be an option. There would be no marketing budget. I would be on my own.

The First Forty Years
of McCabe Pilgrimages

McCABE TRAVEL

37A WALDRON ROAD LONDON SW18 3TB ENGLAND   TEL 01-947 8301   TELEX 291829 ATTN "MCCABE"

LIFE & WORK
FEBRUARY 1983

INDIA
KATHMANDU and the
HIMALAYAS

November 15 days

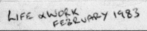

The REVD JAMES CURRIE and the REVD GEORGE McCABE will
be leading this tour to the land of Gandhi, visiting the Taj Mahal,
Ganges River and the Himalayan Kingdom of Nepal on the roof of
the World.

Join them for THE experience of 1983! Full details and brochure
now available from:

McCABE TRAVEL

37A Waldron Road, London SW18.
Telephone (01) 947 8301

FIRST
BOOKING!

38 Station Rd
Dunure
Ayr KA7 4LL
9/2/83

Mr A. McCabe
McCabe Travel
37a Waldron Road
LONDON S.W. 18.

Dear Mr McCabe, We received your letter
of 7th Feb. giving details of the following
tour   India, Kathmandu & Himalayas
November 12-26 1983   Price £850
Leaders Revd. Jas Currie Dunlop
, Revd Geo. McCabe Dalkeith

Please make a firm booking for
two places on this tour in the names
of Robert M. Holms and Jean M. Holms (Note no
Either Holms)
In due course we expect to receive
your brochure (which is presently delayed
at the printers) and other advance
notice regarding deposit etc which we
shall be pleased to attend to promptly.
This visit indeed promises to be a
highlight of 1983   Yours faithfully Jean M Holms

FIRST ENQUIRY !

McCabe Travel

REV A F BOLTON
ARROCHAR MANSE
ARROCHAR
G83 7DE
Dunbartonshire
5/2/83

Dear Sir

Would you please send me
particulars of the 15 Day tour of
India / Kathmandu & Himalaya as
advertised in Life & Work Mag.

Yours truly
Albert F Bolton

ACN'D 10/2.

18

Every good wish to Mc Cabe
Travel and much success in
this new tour operation.
High hopes for a busy, prosperous
and expanding first year.
Kind regards and every good wish
to the proprietors.
Need I say we are always
at your service.

Archie Stewart
Warden

CHURCH OF SCOTLAND HOSPICE
TIBERIAS

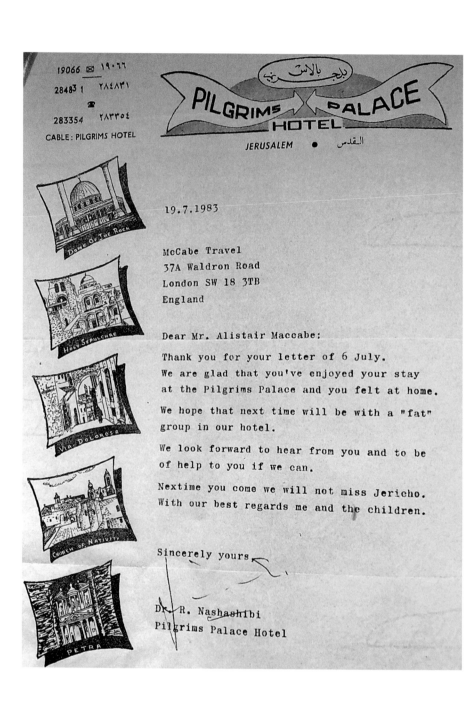

19066 ☒ ١٩٠٦٦
28483 1 ٢٨٤٨٣١
☎
283354 ٢٨٣٣٥٤
CABLE: PILGRIMS HOTEL

PILGRIMS PALACE HOTEL

JERUSALEM • القدس

19.7.1983

McCabe Travel
37A Waldron Road
London SW 18 3TB
England

Dear Mr. Alistair Maccabe:

Thank you for your letter of 6 July.
We are glad that you've enjoyed your stay
at the Pilgrims Palace and you felt at home.

We hope that next time will be with a "fat"
group in our hotel.

We look forward to hear from you and to be
of help to you if we can.

Nextime you come we will not miss Jericho.
With our best regards me and the children.

Sincerely yours,

Dr. R. Nashashibi
Pilgrims Palace Hotel

20

The Early Years
1983 - 1991

McCabe Travel was born in my flat in Earlsfield, bed replaced with sofa bed, desk, chair, filing cabinet, telephone, and typewriter. Flatmates went to work during the day creating office space. McCabe's first employee was Ursula Macleod, Arthur's former secretary and sister-in-law of Lord Macleod, founder of the Iona Community. Ursula had retired from ICT at the same time as Arthur but was still living in London. She came on board and was a solid rock for our first seven years before she retired for a second time in 1990. As a thank you, we gave her a leaving present of a pension for life.

Sadly, Ursula passed away in August 2021 as I am writing this history but even into her nineties, Ursula was always a loyal advocate of McCabe.

The business plan was very basic and could have been written on the back of a cigarette packet. What we did was high risk. We were asking tour leaders to leave the security of a Thomas Cook backed company, for a venture with no track record, no travel licenses, no ABTA membership and offering absolutely no financial security for travellers' funds. (All of the above would be in place within three years). Equally questionable, was whether airlines, hotels, restaurants, guides, and the like would take the risk involved in accepting reservations from a company that may not actually deliver any business or, if they did, be able to pay their bills.

Our start-up capital consisted of a £5,000 gift from hoteliers in Israel, who had been pushing me to start my own venture. I was settling an ICT bill at Motel Canaan in Safed when Moni Shinaar said 'Keep the money and use it to start your own business'. We made this money last a full year before we received our first income. Over the years, the Shinars became family friends and their forward-thinking contribution was repaid many times over.

Appearances are everything! McCabe Travel had a London address, which we, rightly or wrongly, thought gave solidity. I was 'Sole Proprietor', but letterheads and business cards were printed with three directors' names. Bruce was young, about to be ordained and liked to travel (now Revd Dr Canon Bruce Kinsey of Balliol College Oxford). Ursula's 'Macleod of Iona connection' helped, and me. Naivety showed in our first Celtic cross logo being hand drawn on a napkin, and us printing it rough rather than tidying and typesetting the design.

McCabe Travel was not a Limited Company. No lawyers were involved. It was established that I could use my own name without a problem, there was no requirement for any travel licences and booking conditions were largely copied from Thomas Cook. It's hard to believe now how much trust there was involved. The only professional contribution was from Mr Blogg (real name) Barclays Earlsfield Bank Manager. With his help we got our first cheque book – but no overdraft!

We wrote a letter to all the clergy that between us we knew, introducing the company, and Ursula and I did a tour visiting many of them. I was accused of stealing the address details of ICT leaders. Nonsense of course, as many were friends and clergy contact details are in the public domain. The biggest factor in getting the company off the ground was the encouragement and support of three Scottish pilgrimage organisers: Rev James Currie, Rev Moses Donaldson, and Rev Effie Irvine (Britain's first female minister to have her own parish). My family were reticent. I was leaving a good job and they were very aware that I had extremely limited funds.

Our First Year

Our £5,000 start-up funding was budgeted to last a year. We spent this on advertising, initial brochures, travel wallets, luggage labels, a 'Brother' typewriter, telephone, paper, etc and living expenses, including running a cheap car - not so easy nowadays with the cost of insurance.

The business plan consisted of selling a high profile, income-generating first tour within our first year of operation, creating enough cash to fund a further year. In our second year, we would operate our first series of Holy Land tours, producing funds for a third year, and so on. We had no real picture of how long it would take to become a viable company. Key was keeping overheads as low as possible, staying single with no family responsibilities and being willing to work seven days a week.

The first months were strange. There was no routine, no office to go to and very little actual work to do. We didn't have computers or the internet to fill our time, and the phone didn't ring. The money worry was constant, and I can remember getting quite depressed at times. My flat had connections with Earlsfield Baptist Church and I started attending. I met a great group of people who enjoyed each other's company, and they helped me regain a positive attitude. By Easter, the mood had changed and we were busy!

Rev James Currie had always wanted to visit India and was happy to invite his regular travellers. This combined with the McCabe family's long missionary association with India, was the starting point for our first McCabe pilgrimage, a 'meet the people' tour of India and Nepal. James would co-lead with my father, George, and the tour would be that November, an ideal month weather-wise but a very short selling period. However, we needed the revenue from this one holiday in 1983 to provide funds to survive into 1984.

February 1983, a single advert in the Church of Scotland magazine *Life & Work*, plus James's promotion, produced seventy firm bookings. We were immediately toast-of-the-town with the Indian tourist office!

March 1983, we launched our first brochure of Holy Land pilgrimages with Inter Church leaders transferring their allegiance and providing the backbone. James Currie and Effie Irvine travelled every year with ninety pilgrims. Moses Donaldson was charismatic and a great recruiter. My father invited the then Moderator of the Church of Scotland, Andrew Doig, to co-lead a pilgrimage at Easter. Bruce organised a party. Known pilgrimage leaders were invited to take pilgrimages, in the hope that they would fill their parties from their own contacts. Three months after launching, our first booking forms and cheque deposits started coming in. These reservations were confirmed by Ursula on our one typewriter. Tour Leaders were phoning us to discuss itineraries. We tried to avoid anyone coming to the flat, so I would drive to meet leaders in their homes or arrange a meeting in central London. Thomas Cook had a reputation as the best training ground in travel and our early systems were unashamedly copied from Cooks. When I retired from McCabe, the booking model in use was the one I copied from Thomas Cook in our first year.

We benefitted from Inter Church Travel losing its personal touch and more ICT regular leaders contacted us. We were accused of stealing business, but group organisers are free to travel with whoever they choose, and our success has been built on the fact that over 37 years, very few pilgrimage organisers have left McCabe to travel with other companies.

We started something new – a brochure promoting do-it-yourself holidays for couples or families staying in Christian guest houses in Jerusalem and Tiberias. This idea never really took off, but it was invaluable in building relationships between the new company and the Christian community in the Holy Land.

The first year was financially very difficult. We were receiving deposits for future tours, but there would be no earned income until November, and only then if our first tour to India and Nepal was a success.

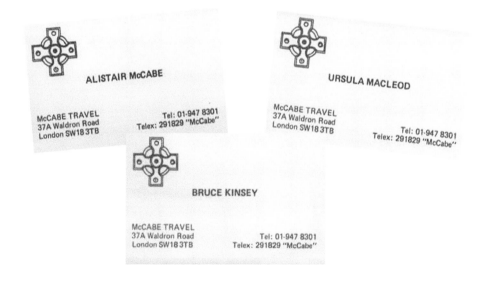

ALISTAIR McCABE

McCABE TRAVEL
37A Waldron Road
London SW18 3TB

Tel: 01-947 8301
Telex: 291829 "McCabe"

URSULA MACLEOD

McCABE TRAVEL
37A Waldron Road
London SW18 3TB

Tel: 01-947 8301
Telex: 291829 "McCabe"

BRUCE KINSEY

McCABE TRAVEL
37A Waldron Road
London SW18 3TB

Tel: 01-947 8301
Telex: 291829 "McCabe"

McCABE TRAVEL

INDIA KATHMANDU AND THE HIMALAYAS

12-26 NOVEMBER 1983

The Revd James Currie

The Revd George McCabe

We were fortunate to have a high-profile event ready to go. My family have been missionaries in India for three generations and in 1983 tourism to India and Nepal was still quite small, and it was the Rev James Currie's lifetime ambition to travel there.

My father and James led the tour, assisted by myself and a local tour manager, Jayant Karambelkar. We put together a programme visiting big attractions like the Taj Mahal, the Delhi of the British Raj and legendary Kathmandu and combined this with looking at how Indian life differed from our own. George spoke Hindi, so we would stop at a random village in the countryside and walk through, introducing the group to the rural India that makes up most of the country, and discussing the difference between the poverty of the city slum dwellers and the lives of villagers, who had very little, but enough. Beggars were a constant in the city but, in the villages, we were never asked for money. I have a memory of James, in his kilt, walking on his own through a village of mud huts, deep in thought. These encounters had a very unsettling effect on James and many of the group, so far out of their comfort zone.

Flying into Varanasi, the Hindu holy city on the Ganges was a culture shock. Jayant, our tour manager had become an integral part of our group, and it was his initiative for us to save our airline meal, and hand out seventy boxes to a needy community on arrival.

Nowhere in India is the contrast between Christianity and Hinduism so stark, as in Varanasi. We rose at dawn and sailed on the river watching the faithful bathing in the holy waters with cremation pyres on the riverbank and ashes and orange puja flowers floating by - seventy Scottish pilgrims were in the middle of an alien universe.

When we shared in worship with a local Christian congregation, our group left an offering of more than their annual income and the pastor insisted we write an explanation, in case the authorities asked where the money had come from. The amount was not large but humbling as our own standard of living was highlighted.

We left the plains of India and flew to Kathmandu, a short flight into a different world. Nepal only opened its doors to visitors in the 1950s, when my grandfather was one of the first missionaries to cross the Bagmati River into the 'forbidden' kingdom. Because of this separation, Nepal is very different to India, with its cultural influences coming from China and Tibet. We explored a city of intricately carved medieval buildings and pagodas overlooked by the awe-inspiring Himalayas. We discovered tolerance in religion with a Buddhism which had incorporated many Hindu traits, a softer, more accommodating religion than the fervour of Varanasi. Friends from the United Mission to Nepal joined us and gave us an insight into the challenges faced by the few Christians living here.

This first McCabe tour set the pattern for the future. We would focus on a group experience, visiting iconic places, engaging with the local culture, and our unique McCabe aspect would be our interaction with the local Christian community.

Our First Holy Land Pilgrimage

The American Church in London   February 1984

After the first year, it became clear that larger business premises were required, but with the only actual revenue in the company coming from last year's India tour, and 1984 income still just a promise, money was extremely tight. With the help of a friendly accountant, in July we purchased a dilapidated three-bedroom house not far away, in Tooting. A 110% mortgage was approved, based on projected company profitability. In addition, we received a 90% grant from the council for the renovation work. The house had no central heating or hot water system and very basic plumbing but it was large enough to host an office. Housemates were installed to pay the mortgage and the public areas during the day became the McCabe office for the next four years. The staff expanded to four with the arrival of an old school friend, Anne Wright, and Kit Turnbull, our first salesperson.

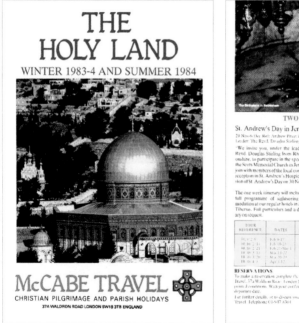

Our very first Holy Land pilgrimage travelled on 9 February 1984 and was with a completely new client. The Revd Ron Allison, head of the American Church in London, heard what we were doing and, 38 years on, Ron keeps in touch from his retirement home in the States having organised all his church pilgrimages through McCabe.

It had taken a year but Inter Church Travel now responded to the threat we posed. James Currie had led forty previous pilgrimages with Inter Church and they were not happy losing a prime customer. ICT gave their partners in the Holy Land an ultimatum. They could either continue working with Inter Church or work with Alistair, but not both. James rose above this and accepted that Joseph Aweidah would no longer be his partner and that his parties could no longer stay at the Panorama Hotel. James's regular guide, Hamid, chose to work with McCabe, as did Nazareth Coach Company and the Scottie in Tiberias.

We had an immediate problem as our Jerusalem hotel reservations were cancelled at short notice. Dr Rashid Nashashibi believed in us and took the opportunity to bring the first McCabe groups to the then Pilgrims Palace (now Golden Walls) Hotel, initiating a family and business friendship which still stands today. Fahmi, Rashid's son, is now approaching retirement after looking after McCabe clients in his hotel for the past 37 years. Cementing the friendship, Fahmi's daughter Nada became a key McCabe staff member in London for ten years. This is a picture showing the four generations of the Nashashibi family, that I have been privileged to know.

Joseph Aweidah was apologetic for letting us down, but we found the perfect new Holy Land partner in Francois Albina, proprietor of his family business, Albina Tours. Francois looked after several upmarket British tour companies including Bales, Abercrombie & Kent, and Jasmin (which McCabe would later purchase).

The problem for Francois was that each of these companies would typically bring only two or three small parties annually to Jerusalem and Francois realised that McCabe had the potential to be the larger partner that the Albina business needed. It was Jim Smith of Jasmin who introduced me to Francois and we hit it off immediately.

Sadly, Francois died in 1989 aged only 58, leaving his wife Vehanoush and three young children. Vehanoush had never worked in the office, but stepped up, learned quickly, and took over the reins. I met 21-year-old Natasha for the first time at her father's bedside. Francois had very much wanted us to meet. Natasha remembers the first words I said to her, 'you are the girl I send all the money to'. Our groups had been paying for her education in America. Natasha's younger brother joined the company from university but sadly he too succumbed to illness and passed away in 2017 aged only 46. Today, Vehanoush at 84 still holds the reins, ably supported by Natasha and Walid Naber, who has been core office staff since the time of Francois. We are privileged to have another partner family in Jerusalem who, for 37 years, have looked after McCabe travellers with unparalleled care and attention.

Our partnerships with the Albina and Nashashibi families formed so many years ago are the bedrock of McCabe Holy Land pilgrimages today.

In our second year we looked after twenty pilgrimages and 500 travellers. We had survived two years living on a shoestring and had built up capital in terms of satisfied clients and tour leaders and now had a business track record, which opened the doors to an overdraft and suppliers confident to give us credit.

Developing New Destinations   1985

Greece and Turkey

The early years of McCabe were very much Holy Land pilgrimage based, except for our niche market India adventures. In 1985 we developed a tour through Greece following St Paul's missionary journeys. I look back fondly on our early itinerary because it was so much fun. We included stays on the Greek islands of Patmos and Samos and a day trip from Samos to Ephesus in Turkey.

The journey from Athens to Patmos was by the regular passenger steamer, and we travelled without the coach, and baggage handling was a nightmare. For the second sail from Patmos to Samos we chartered a local caique for the three-hour sail. In good weather, this was magnificent, (the picture above shows me with Tour Leader, Revd Paul Rees on this crossing and, in the background in white, 'Mrs Mary' from Tiberias days) but in bad weather, a long arduous crossing. Our itinerary ended with us flying home from Samos, via Athens, which meant we had to cross to Samos whatever the weather, small boat being the only option, to connect with this flight. Greece and Turkey have long disputed the ownership of islands like Samos, which lie very close to the Turkish coast and the formalities of arranging our day trip to Ephesus were longwinded including needing to obtain Turkish visas.

Paul and I helping the staff at our Patmos hotel

Moses Donaldson led one of our early trips and his experience was typical of how often things going wrong became tour highlights. These were days before mobile phones and communication on a complicated itinerary such as this, often broke down. The passenger steamer arrived on the island of Patmos at midnight after an eight-hour sail, only to find the hotel was not expecting the group till the following night, and they were full. Moses had befriended a lorry driver on the ferry, delivering mattresses to the island. The mattresses were commandeered and laid out around the hotel corridors, and after a short night's sleep, rooms were available the next morning. On the same trip, the party sailing by small boat from Patmos to Samos, were met on arrival, but we lost communication with them between port and hotel. It was now dark, and we were concerned. Later, we found out the story. The coach had broken down in a remote location and Moses, instead of worrying, took the opportunity to hold a Communion Service as the sun set over the Mediterranean. For the party, this was the highlight of the trip.

Over the years, we developed our Pauline journeys, creating itineraries in Greece and Turkey but, instead of using regular ferries and small boats, we incorporated the more secure option of three nights on a cruise ship visiting Patmos and Ephesus. Later, Turkey would become a principal destination with multiple itineraries featuring St Paul's Journeys, the Seven Churches of Revelation, and the History of the Early Church.

The Pilgrim Fathers

McCabe Travel was built on the knowledge, experience, and enthusiasm of a few pilgrimage organisers extraordinaire. The Rev James Currie organised 46 Holy Land pilgrimages, and McCabe was privileged to be his partner for the last four years of his life. I travelled on all his McCabe ventures, trying to introduce James to new ideas, but mostly accepting that James did things his way. I learnt more from James, than James learned from me.

For James, repetition was the key. The itinerary did not change, and at every site, restaurant, shop, and hotel, he knew the staff by name, and he always had the same guide and coach driver. Many of his pilgrims came on multiple trips and they became part of a close-knit and warm family. Worship was serious and sincere, but coach journeys were a riot of fun, with James giving a running commentary, telling stories, joking, and leading the singing. Always wearing a kilt, James would wade into the Jordan River and conduct full immersion baptisms. Evenings would be filled with moonlit walks from Gethsemane to the Upper Room, local Christians telling their story, ceilidhs and folklore shows. Sunday worship at the Scottish Kirk in Jerusalem and Tiberias was a must, with James usually conducting the services.

We were 'Scotland on Tour' and would visit Tabeetha, the Church of Scotland school in Jaffa and the Edinburgh Medical Missionary Society hospital in Nazareth. In Tiberias, we stayed at the Scottie, today the deluxe Scots Hotel, but then a Guest House but with a great history and lakeside location. James didn't believe in free time. His mantra was 'You can sleep when you get home'. We sang the 'Scottish' Psalm, The Lord's my Shepherd, everywhere we went, and regularly joined in the Lord's Prayer. We would often have visitors on the coach, be it Scottish missionaries or hitchhikers on the road. Whoever it was would be given the microphone to tell their story. James had very little time for the history of places, dates, or architecture and he avoided politics.

We were on a pilgrimage. Our guide was there for logistical reasons, sat at the back of the bus and wasn't given the microphone!

The one negative with James was that he was not a listener and he led from the front at his pace. A typical pilgrimage would have ninety participants. Revd Effie Irvine would follow James on the second bus, often accompanied by James' wife, Peggy, and me. In the days before mobile phones, we had to guess where James was going next. In conversation with an ex-serviceman, James had changed the morning's programme and we were now going to have a service at the Commonwealth War Graves on the Mount of Olives, or lunch scheduled for noon was now changed to one o'clock. Walking in the Old City, it was the task of the guide and co-leaders to shepherd the flock in the general right direction. Peggy and Effie were light heartedly

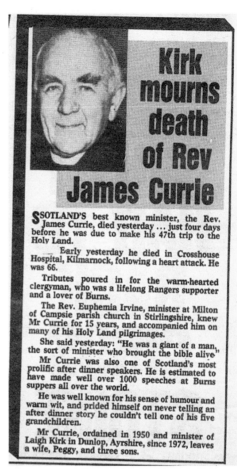

Kirk mourns death of Rev James Currie

SSOTLAND'S best known minister, the Rev. James Currie, died yesterday ... just four days before he was due to make his 47th trip to the Holy Land.

Early yesterday he died in Crosshouse Hospital, Kilmarnock, following a heart attack. He was 66.

Tributes poured in for the warm-hearted clergyman, who was a lifelong Rangers supporter and a lover of Burns.

The Rev. Euphemia Irvine, minister at Milton of Campsie parish church in Stirlingshire, knew Mr Currie for 15 years, and accompanied him on many of his Holy Land pilgrimages.

She said yesterday: "He was a giant of a man, the sort of minister who brought the bible alive"

Mr Currie was also one of Scotland's most prolific after dinner speakers. He is estimated to have made well over 1000 speeches at Burns suppers all over the world.

He was well known for his sense of humour and warm wit, and prided himself on never telling an after dinner story he couldn't tell one of his five grandchildren.

Mr Currie, ordained in 1950 and minister of Laigh Kirk in Dunlop, Ayrshire, since 1972, leaves a wife, Peggy, and three sons.

constantly blaming me for not controlling James, something neither of them had ever succeeded in doing.

I learnt that pilgrimage is not about places, it's about people. People from all walks of life joined a James Currie pilgrimage. A typical pilgrim would be a single woman, many widowed with limited means, living on her own. An annual or bi-annual pilgrimage with James was something she saved up for, and for two weeks she would be part of an extended family giving new energy and meaning to her life. Church going wives would be accompanied by reluctant husbands and it was exciting to see the ice melt as the men were drawn into the experience. A party would also be a mix of regulars and newcomers, but it was remarkable how very different people quickly bonded as a 'Currie' group.

Each day, the excitement would be to meet locals who had become friends, as they visited familiar restaurants, shops, and holy places. Many of James's people were more comfortable in the Holy Land than back at home in Scotland.

James died on 18 April 1987, a few days before a pilgrimage. Effie and other leaders would continue the tradition for a while, but the reality was that the James Currie type of pilgrimage was coming to an end. An aging clientele, meant that most of these people simply stopped travelling, leaving, I suspect, a big hole in their lives – like it did for all of us at McCabe Travel. James was a giant of a man, in more ways than one, and lived his life to the full, with many strings to his bow. (William Coffey's excellent biography is worth reading) It was a privilege to be part of his inner circle. McCabe Travel's success was built on the strong foundation of genuine trust of tour leaders for many of whom pilgrimage was central to their ministry. I have always regarded it an honour to be a part of the life of people like James.

Our start-up capital was people. The Rev Moses Donaldson had been a coal miner before 'coming to Christ' at a Billy Graham crusade and being ordained into the Church of Scotland ministry. The first time we met, Moses asked me if he could lead a pilgrimage to Jordan, despite the fact he had never visited himself. My reply that the first Moses hadn't been their either, amused him. Moses would go on to lead more than fifty McCabe pilgrimages to every destination we offered, including an early trip to the Scottish island of Iona which, thirty years later, would become a central itinerary on our 'Short Breaks' initiative.

When my father died, Moses inherited his robes, which he wore when conducting my wedding. Moses could live in the moment, something I have always found hard to do. Visiting the Taj Mahal, Moses persuaded me to step away from the party to have our photograph taken on the famous 'Princess Diana' bench. I was reluctant as my mind, as always, was on the thirty travellers with us. It was a valuable lesson, to seize the moment - it won't come again.

I spoke at Rev Effie Irvine's 90th birthday celebration, an opportunity to recall stories from the exactly fifty pilgrimages she conducted with McCabe. From the very beginning, when we would be on the second bus following James around Jerusalem, to Nile cruises and trekking in the Himalayas. She often co-led with my father, and they are pictured here hosting fancy dress night on a Nile cruise.

Effie, Moses, James, and my father were typical Scottish ministers of the time. Their ministries were people based and regular visiting of the congregation was central. They got to know the families in their congregation, whether they attended church or not. This I had a huge respect for.

Pilgrimage for them was an extension of their ministry. The Gospel is a powerful story, especially told in the places where Jesus lived. Effie, James, Moses, my father, and so many leaders like them, never tired of visiting The Holy Land and bringing to life familiar Bible stories in situ. I regard it a huge privilege to have shared so many pilgrimages with tour leaders like these and the pilgrims who travelled with them. Without their inspiration, McCabe Travel would never have succeeded.

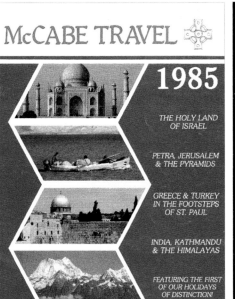

McCABE TRAVEL

1985

THE HOLY LAND
OF ISRAEL

PETRA, JERUSALEM
& THE PYRAMIDS

GREECE & TURKEY
IN THE FOOTSTEPS
OF ST. PAUL

INDIA, KATHMANDU
& THE HIMALAYAS

FEATURING THE FIRST
OF OUR HOLIDAYS
OF DISTINCTION!

CHRISTIAN TRAVEL AND HOLIDAYS

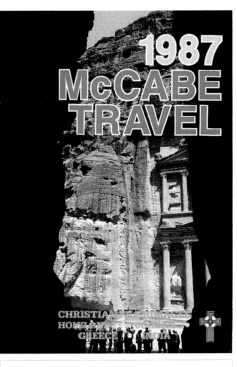

1987 McCABE TRAVEL

CHRISTIAN
HOLY
GREECE AND INDIA

McCABE TRAVEL 1988

THE HOLY LAND JORDAN
ST PAUL IN GREECE AND TURKEY
EXPERIENCE INDIA

McCABE TRAVEL 1989

BRITAIN'S FOREMOST RELIGIOUS TOUR OPERATOR

THE HOLYLAND
OBERAMMERGAU
JOURNEYS OF ST. PAUL

Early Staffing

The early staffing of McCabe was largely friends joining the team. Ursula and I worked alone for the first year, with friends Anne Wright and Kit Turnbull then joining.

In 1987 the future shape of the company was put in place when Kit and Jane were married and returned to New Zealand. In a casual conversation, my friend Bill suggested that his younger brother Robert might be interested in a job. Robert joined straight from university in Scotland to work in London. He became a key member of staff over fourteen years and grew our relationship with churches all over the UK.

The culmination of Robert's work was our Millennium project when, in 2000, we organized 24 Diocesan and National pilgrimages to the Holy Land, raising over £500,000 in support of the indigenous Christian community. The company achieved this in parallel with managing a programme of 12,000 travellers to attend the millennium Oberammergau Passion Play – but we are getting ahead of our story.

Pictured above are Kit Turnbull at CRE. Robert Trimble. Rosemary with Arthur Payton. Overleaf: Rosemary with Marlene Nashashibi. Norma Finnegan and Dave Lunn.

In the same year, Rosemary Nutt joined us after graduating with a degree in music. Rosemary's father had been a director of Inter Church Travel and we knew Rosemary from her stints working at Inter Church in the holidays. Apart from a three-year break, Rosemary would be my business partner for the next 35 years. Rosemary managed the finances and travel operations, organising air tickets and documentation for each pilgrimage.

Robert was our main contact with church leaders, and I focused on running the business and future planning. We now had a team that was unrivalled among our competitors. The three of us complimented each other in our skills and church affiliation with Rosemary and Robert attending very different kinds of churches and me maintaining my Baptist and Church of Scotland affiliations. We prided ourselves that between us, we would personally know each Tour Leader and each of us would build and develop that relationship.

With Oberammergau on the horizon, family friend Philip Alford joined and would be our representative in Austria during the 1990 Passion Play season. In our first foray away from family friends, we recruited two staff from our rival Inter church Travel and, in 1989, Fiona Dewar and Norma Finnegan joined the team. We thank Fiona for introducing us to, among others, Geoffrey Marshall and Paul Miller, group organisers who became part of the fabric of McCabe. Ursula retired in February 1990, with the company firmly established and ready for our first Oberammergau season.

Creating McCabe Travel Ltd in 1987

In 1987 we became McCabe Travel Ltd, joined ABTA, provided full financial protection for our clients' money and we moved into our first dedicated office premises, 59 Balham Hill, near Clapham Common. This was an object lesson in how not to rent a property. I viewed the premises a few times, but always in the morning. When we moved in, the significance of the betting shop below became clear. Horse racing commentary was live fed every afternoon and upstairs we heard it loud and clear. Each month I received the rent demand from our bookie landlord on a betting slip with the rent listed under 'You Lose!'. The company moved office three times but has stayed within five minutes' walk of that initial decision.

The 1980s was a period of rapid technological change. Looking back, the speed was staggering. Typewriter became electric typewriter, which Ursula hated because the keys moved too fast. Tippex was an essential - a typing mistake meant you either painted over it or started again. Photocopiers existed, but they were expensive and only black and white. When we started out in 1982, we used carbon paper to make copies, and the simplest of leaflets had to be printed professionally. Airlines would supply us glossy paper with colour destination pictures, and we would fill the spaces with our holiday details, producing cheap colour brochures.

We purchased a Fax machine in 1986 and I remember big discussions with Gazi at Nazareth Coach Company as to whether it was worth buying one. (Incidentally, vinyl records moved to CDs in 1985) We bought our first Amstrad computer in 1988, which crashed continually. Mobile phones came on the scene, but they were suitcase size. Phone calls were very expensive, especially international ones, so most communication at the beginning was by post with typically a three-week turnaround for a request to Israel.

Team Building

A fun thing we did as a company was introduce an annual staff team building exercise. For four years in a row, we visited one of our key destinations, and tried to do something a little different. We chose the first week in December as a quiet week in the office and a cheap time to travel.

Our first venture was to the Galilee where we white-water rafted on the Jordan River. We started off with a safety exercise of floating down the river without the raft, which set the tone for an exhilarating experience well out of most of our comfort zones. We were joined by our partners in Israel, and it was a great success.

In the following years, we travelled together to Malta, Istanbul and sailed on the Nile. Our picture shows Joan, Stuart, Ben and John enjoying the Nile cruise fancy dress evening.

Our staff pic on the Jordan River: Lori, Alistair, Ben, Rosemary, Anne, Stuart and Rob and front row Tony Albina, Andy, Mark and our loyal McCabe guide Oliver Miller.

The staged photo opposite shows my father and his brother Andrew and my mother.

Our Gap Year India Project

'Experience India' was a project that ran for four years under the direction of Canon Kenneth Jones and Revd Bruce Kinsey. We took gap year students on a three-week tour of India then arranged a volunteer placement for three months, placing students with Mother Theresa in Calcutta, my uncle Andrew McCabe's mission near Lucknow, and at various schools throughout India. It was a real privilege for these students to meet Mother Theresa and work alongside her Sisters of Mercy helping provide care and daily meals for the destitute in Calcutta.

Pictured above, Bruce with our first Experience India group of students

Not Just a Travel Company

McCabe is a company with a strong Christian ethos, but our staff have always been a mix of churchgoers and not. From a neutral starting point, we create pilgrimage itineraries in tune with the priorities of each partner church and we have tried to recruit staff who understand this. I valued the occasions when pilgrimage leaders shared with us concerns and problems in their parish lives. This trust was special, and I think made easier by the fact we did not identify with any one branch of the church. We encouraged different churches to work together, and highlights have been ecumenical projects, bringing together churches that would normally have quite separate lives. Pilgrimage breaks down barriers, and differences which appear large at home, are put in perspective travelling together with a common purpose.

'Know your neighbour' grew into an ever more important theme, as we encouraged British church goers of all denominations to meet fellow Christians overseas. We built fund-raising partnerships with the Scottish hospital in Nazareth and the Blind School in Bethlehem. When James Currie died in 1987, we raised funds for a Chapel to be built in his memory at the Scottie in Tiberias. Glasgow Rangers Football Club contributed the Communion silverware and Nazareth Coach company a beautifully carved wooden altar.

A natural progression was the McCabe Educational Trust, which we set up in 1990 as a vehicle to make it easy for our travellers to financially support less well-off Christian communities that we met on our travels.

We saw ourselves as part of the church's ministry and not just a travel company. Arthur Payton had been fiercely ecumenical, and McCabe followed this path, respecting all Christian traditions and tailor-making each pilgrimage itinerary. Not aligning the company with any one denomination has, I think, been an important part of our success. We understood the needs of High Anglican, Baptist, Methodist or Church of Scotland congregations, and respected each approach equally.

Pictured is a McCabe pilgrim receiving a gift from Israeli Prime Minister, Shimon Peres, marking the one millionth visitor to Israel.

Clergy Introductory Tours

Few churches went on a Holy Land pilgrimage at this time. One initiative was to invite clergy to come and see 'The Land' for themselves on a one-week taster tour and then encourage them to take their own church on pilgrimage. The idea was not new, but our approach was to treat each trip as a pilgrimage and potentially a ministry-changing experience as, for most, this would be their first visit to the Holy Land.

A theme of an early pilgrimage was 'how a Holy Land pilgrimage can transform you and your church'. My father led some of these partnered by Robert Llewelyn, an Anglican clergyman from Gloucester, and great McCabe supporter. (Later his son Ben would join McCabe and manage our 1990 Oberammergau coach programme). They were poles apart in their approach to pilgrimage and Christianity in general, but that helped set the tone and emphasized that McCabe was not part of any one branch of the church. These pilgrimages were the closest we came to Arthur's ecumenical dream, and I still think our biggest contribution to the life of the church.

Revd Peter Hall (centre front) and guide Rami (kneeling on left) with Lynne standing on the right and a typical clergy introductory tour, pictured at the Holy Sepulchre.

We would use different denominational liturgy at different sites. A Church of Scotland Holy Communion service would be very different from an Anglican Eucharist. Some participants came with closed minds and belittled others' churchmanship, but for most this was a time to appreciate and gain understanding of the church's many different approaches and expressions of a common faith. On a more personal level, participants valued the opportunity to share in confidence worries and concerns of parish life. Some of course just came for the cheap holiday and we were happy for them to enjoy a week's respite from an often-stressful parish situation.

Our Holy Land partners co-operated, and we were able to offer these trips at low cost. A big incentive to the participants was, that if they planned their own parish pilgrimage in the future, we would refund the introductory pilgrimage cost. One January, we took 200 clergy on a series of these pilgrimages. These experiences were our principal promotional tool in bringing new group organisers to McCabe.

Our idea was developed by some Anglican dioceses, and we ran joint ventures as part of their Post Ordination Training programme. The budget for these trips was shared between the diocese and McCabe as we hoped that some of these new clergy would become future pilgrimage leaders. I would like to see a Holy land pilgrimage becoming integral to all clergy training. They will learn more from a week in situ than a month in the classroom.

Christian Resources Exhibition

We participated in the first Christian Resources Exhibition and the McCabe stand became a regular CRE fixture. At the first exhibition our stand was in darkness as we hadn't bought the 'extras' package, including lighting. We had taken our own furniture from the office. We soon realised it was easier and cheaper to rent from the exhibition support staff. There was much naivety in the beginning, and we learned from our mistakes.

In 1989, Arthur Payton was part of our hosting team and Sybille joined us from Salzburg. We invited Adi and Ingrid Thum, woodcarvers from Oberammergau who carved a beautiful Madonna on the stand during the four days of the exhibition, creating great interest in what was to be the first of four McCabe Oberammergau seasons.

Another year, we made the mistake of offering wine and snacks and, looking at the stand from a distance, I realised that our full stand comprised people we knew. Good PR, but very few new contacts.

CRE was a great meeting place and helped put our name on the map, but we found that very little actual business was done. We pulled out, but I am pleased the new management of McCabe has re-joined.

McCabe Wanderers FC

Earlsfield Baptist Church in south London played a big part in our growing company, particularly Percy and Maureen Sore, senior members, who took me under their wing. Maureen joined our team and for many years was our only computer literate person. Pastor Arthur Robinson became a Tour Leader and friendships in the church led to Jackie joining the company. Jackie's future husband, David Humphries, started a church football team – which McCabe Travel sponsored.

We played ad hoc games against other church teams, which led to an initiative from Revd Gary Piper, chaplain of Fulham football club, and goalkeeper of the St Matthew's team, to start the McCabe South London Christian Football League. Myself, David, Robert Trimble, and his brother Bill played in the McCabe Wanderers team. Many players in the league had no church connection and Gary valued the opportunity to share his faith. An annual Presentation Dinner was held and one year we had Allan Mullery (former Fulham player and England captain) presenting the McCabe sponsored awards.

During the 1990 Oberammergau season, I discovered a black hole on our charter flight schedule, with thirty unsold places for two weeks' time. McCabe Wanderers enjoyed their first European tour to Austria! Flights were complimentary, accommodation subsidised, and matches arranged by McCabe's local reps. Team, wives and girlfriends went on tour, lost all the matches, and had a great time.

Adding a bit of historical perspective, in 1988 our local team Wimbledon won the FA Cup, beating European champions, Liverpool in the biggest giant killing act since David! Most of the McCabe team were at the match. A memorable Wembley day out.

First Intifada In The Middle East 1987 - 1991

It didn't take long before the reality of working with the Middle East kicked in. The first Intifada (Palestinian uprising) against the Israeli occupation began in 1987 and persisted for almost five years, finally ending in 1991 with the Madrid Peace Conference. The Oslo Accords of 1993 followed with the still unfulfilled promise of a two-state solution. The Palestinian resistance was largely confined to stone throwing, but sadly more than a thousand Palestinians and two hundred Israelis lost their lives. Tourism to Israel continued during this period but, understandably, many churches were reluctant to travel on pilgrimage. I remember discussing the situation with Ahmed Affifi, owner of Nazareth Coach Company, and he assured me that as an Israeli-Arab company their coaches would not be a target. An additional precaution was to put a brightly coloured red and white keffiyeh on the front of each coach.

During this time, Israeli coaches would not enter Bethlehem, but we would enter using a side route or change coaches at the border and use a Bethlehem coach to visit the Church of the Nativity. In addition, many protests were planned events and our network of partners would know times and places and we would change itineraries at short notice to avoid trouble spots. Even today, we take our parties out of Jerusalem on a Friday, as noon Friday Prayers on the Temple Mount are a regular flashpoint.

The Golden Walls Hotel, our base in Jerusalem, is on the Palestinian side of the city as are most of the Holy Places we visit, and very few Israelis ventured here during this time so, again, we were not a target and our people were well looked after and felt secure. Tiberias, being a wholly Jewish city, was not affected by the uprising, so pilgrim groups at the Scottie or Ron Beach Hotel were unaffected by the unrest. Occasionally, mistakes happened and stones were thrown, but none of our travellers were hurt during these long four years.

I think, in the early years, our clients were perhaps more trusting than now, the thinking being that they were on an organised holiday, therefore safe. Litigation was also rare. Over the years, itineraries have become much less adventurous as tolerance of things going off plan has reduced, and a lot of the spontaneity and fun of the early days has diminished because of this.

Our Only Serious Accident in 1990

As I write the history of 37 years of McCabe Pilgrimages, we have only had one serious coach accident, which came in our early years, November 1990. The first rains had hit Jerusalem and our coach was heading to Jericho. It overturned in the slippery conditions - sadly one woman died and twenty travellers were hospitalised.

This is when the importance of friends, goodwill and insurance come in to play. Everybody played their part. The Albina family co-ordinated locally, McCabe Educational Trust director, Revd David Praill, flew to Jerusalem and Robert and Rosemary contacted relatives. Insurance companies of the coach company, McCabe and of the travellers involved co-operated with each other. The bill was enormous covering hospitalisation and air ambulance repatriation to the UK. Today, we are aware of what can happen, and take safety and insurance very seriously. Robert and I attended the funeral at the Salvation Army citadel in Oxford and Major Joyce Dixon, the group leader, was very grateful for all that was done. Joyce continued to lead pilgrimages to the Holy Land with us.

Robert Trimble advises on a Holy Land tour.

Alistair McCabe Managing Director The Revd George McCabe Director

Robert Trimble } Tours Managers
Fiona Dewar

Rosemary Nutt Office Manager

Ursula Macleod }
Norma Finnegan } Administration
Philip Alford

McCabe Travel, 53-55 Balham Hill, London SW12 9DR Reservations 01-675 6828

51

Oberammergau 1990

In 1984 we had the opportunity to participate in a special 'between the decades' season of Oberammergau Passion Plays, celebrating the 350th anniversary of the first performances, and making up for the only time the play was cancelled, which was in 1940 during World War II. I think we took the wise decision not to be involved as the company was less than a year old and we lacked almost everything to undertake such a large and risky venture. But this was another hurdle for us, as some Inter Church travel leaders would travel to the Holy Land with us and to Oberammergau with Inter Church – James Currie amongst them. What I hadn't fully appreciated was that Inter Church, under new management, would also be new to Oberammergau. I think the experience of leaders dealing with both companies simultaneously did us a lot of good.

Six years later, 1990 was to be the first of four McCabe Oberammergau seasons and each one was to present serious challenges. Our first season was our most difficult as we were caught up in a ticket scandal, but managing this crisis successfully gave the company a new strength.

But first, a bit of history, going back to 1633 and a village in southern Germany, near the Austrian border. Quoting from Canon Peter Nicholson's words in the McCabe brochure:

'Towards the end of the Thirty Years' War in Central Europe there was an outbreak of the plague in Bavaria. The elders of the village of Oberammergau, to protect their village, decided to seal it off from outside contact. But an itinerant worker returned, bringing the plague with him, and it swept through the village. The people vowed that, if God would show compassion and lift the scourge, they would enact, every ten years, the momentous events of Holy Week from Palm Sunday to Easter Monday.

The plague left the village and, as a perpetual thanksgiving and re-affirmation of faith, the villagers of Oberammergau have performed the Passion Play at ten year intervals ever since'.

Originally on a small scale, in the 1950s attending the play became an iconic thing to do. Today, the auditorium seats close to 4,500 people and there are 100 performances during a twenty week summer season. In the biggest scene, a thousand villagers re-create Palm Sunday on the open-air stage with another 400 involved backstage or in the choir and orchestra. The remarkable fact is that all the participants, including the director, orchestra, choir, and principal players, were either born in the village or have lived there for twenty years. The standard is professional.

In the 1950s, it wasn't easy to travel independently to Oberammergau, and something few would contemplate for a one-day performance. Arthur Payton's initiative, with Inter Church Travel, was to make this a group experience and encourage church parties to travel to see the play, combining the performance with a parish holiday in the lakes and mountains of nearby Austria. This combination was given impetus in 1965 when 'The Sound of Music' was filmed in Salzburg and the surrounding lakes.

Inter Church Travel was a principal UK partner of Oberammergau for the 1960, 1970, 1980 and 1984 performances and Arthur was awarded the Gold Medal of Austrian Tourism. McCabe Travel picked up the baton continuing and developing Arthur's initiative for the 1990, 2000, 2010 and shortly the 2022 seasons.

Pictured are Palm Sunday on stage, the auditorium and Arthur receiving his medal

Building a McCabe Oberammergau Team

After an appropriate period from his ICT retirement, Arthur joined McCabe as an advisor and helped us prepare for our first Oberammergau season. We made contacts that would last a lifetime, including Sybille Brunnauer, my partner for three Oberammergau seasons and Albus, the Salzburg coach company now preparing with us for our fourth season in 2022.

At a memorable lunch in Salzburg, Austrian Airlines came on board and Salzburg became our principal airport. We contracted seats on the Thursday scheduled flight from Heathrow and, on Tuesday, we chartered the same plane from Gatwick. Sometimes, it's hard to change a culture and every Tuesday the cabin crew would offer a full plane of McCabe travellers, German newspapers!

Sybille worked for the Salzburger Landesreiseburo, a travel company owned by Raiffeisen Bank, and we signed a contract for them to provide coaching, accommodation, and Passion Play tickets. Sybille found the delightful alpine village of Maria Alm, about an hour's drive from Salzburg, where we contracted three hotels and began a relationship with the village which would last for thirty years.

Pictured centre, Stuart and below Alistair and Rosemary with the Salzburg office team.

A particular pleasure for me was my boss from Tiberias days, Mary Ohannessian, joining us for the season as our representative in Maria Alm. Our team grew with Philip Alford and Sybille's brother Michael becoming our representatives in Austria's Lake District, and Lori, Silke and Angela joining the Salzburg office team.

Our first attempt at a European coach programme was naïve. Elements were good, but we learnt a lot which we would implement in a well-executed coach programme for the 2000 season. In 1990 our driving days were too long and our coaches understaffed. Ten years later, we would add travelling days and a sightseeing programme to the overland journeys and employ a professional tour manager on each coach. The Euro was introduced in 1999, which made the journey across Europe simpler, but in 1990, even going to the toilet en route was complicated, as French Francs would be required, then Deutschmarks, then Austrian Schillings.

Pictured above are Sybille's brother, Michael and Philip. Mary Ohannessian. My father.

Oberammergau Ecumenical Centre

We took over another Arthur Payton initiative. In co-operation with the two Oberammergau churches, the Village Council, the Anglican Diocese of Europe, and other British travel companies, we organised a chaplaincy in the village. The pattern was a Preparatory Meeting on the evening before the play and Open House and a Eucharist after the play. These services were advertised in the official guide to the village and were open to all visitors. The Play is, for many, an intense emotional experience, and the personal counselling services of our team were much used and appreciated.

We rented rooms with a family in the village, seen here with my father and sister, and her children Matthew and Lucy. (Twenty years later in 2010, Matthew would be our representative in the village!) We invited clergy in teams of four to stay for three weeks, with a one week overlap of two leaving and two arriving to give continuity. We called them our rotating vicars. It was regarded as a huge privilege to live in the village for three weeks and the team loved being part of a truly ecumenical set up. Each team comprised a Roman Catholic priest, an Anglican clergyman, and a Free Church minister. Women clergy were still a rarity in 1990, so the fourth member, a woman, was sometimes a nun, or often a lay person.

The chaplains were also the McCabe 'Meet and Greet' team and would look after McCabe guests during their two days' stay in the village. We would repeat this in 2000 but for the 2010 season the concept didn't work for practical reasons. Firstly, the timing of the play changed from an all-day performance to afternoon and evening, and the pattern of most guests being accommodated in the village, changed to more staying in surrounding villages.

A Ticket Scandal

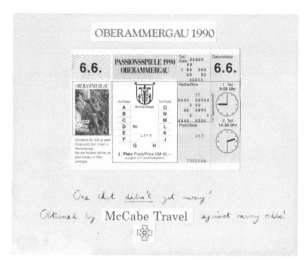

We had successfully recruited 6,000 people to travel in the summer of 1990 and all was in place – or so we thought! A week before the start, we discovered that half of our tickets didn't exist. Other companies were also caught up in what became a major scandal. McCabe's saving grace was that we had purchased our affected tickets through an intermediary bank. Raiffeisen Bank took financial responsibility but, with fully booked performances, they couldn't offer replacement tickets. Sybille and I spent most of the next twenty weeks in the village, procuring black-market tickets, usually at short notice for the following day's performance.

The pressure was intense, and we both grew up quickly. Vlado, a Romanian magician, owned the 'Magic Bar' in the village and this became the unofficial market hub. Somehow, three nights a week for twenty weeks, we managed to buy tickets for the following day's performance. The main ticket source was coaches arriving from all over Europe with empty seats – and spare tickets. On arrival, there would be a scramble to try and acquire these tickets. Our partner bank had the deepest pockets, so we were usually successful. This did not make us popular with other companies in the same situation.

We didn't tell our groups the situation and we also didn't tell our Austrian resort reps, so the morale of parties on holiday was not affected. Sometimes we had to bite our tongue when Philip and Michael asked for time off to go mountain climbing when we were 'climbing the walls' in Oberammergau. We asked affected groups to meet thirty minutes before the performance at the statue of Jesus in front of the theatre, when they would receive their tickets, some of which had been purchased an hour before! We did have complaints from groups not seated together, and some seats were not top grade, but when people came to know the whole story, they were grateful.

One German company went to extreme lengths. In 1990, it was possible to buy a rail ticket from any station in Germany to Oberammergau, including a performance ticket. Travellers took a train to Munich, which connected with an Oberammergau special train which arrived in the village an hour before the day's performance. The travel company, which will remain nameless, purchased rail tickets all over Germany, just for the performance vouchers. The result was a near empty train arriving in Oberammergau some mornings.

Everybody did their best in a bad situation. Couples would share a ticket with one seeing the morning and the other, the afternoon performance. Wheelchair places were abused so the authorities started asking for proof of disability. The Village Council were sympathetic and there was discussion of adding extra performances, but in the end, nothing was done, and everybody somehow found their way through a very stressful season.

Oberammergau 1990 was a life changing experience for all involved. Rosemary stepped up and, in my absence, took control of the London office. There was a feeling that having successfully procured tickets for all our travellers where many other companies had failed, we would manage any crises in the future. Not for the last time, we worked hard, delivered first class holidays but, because of unforeseen crises, received very little financial reward.

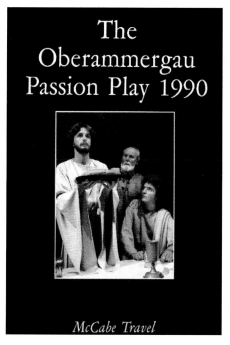

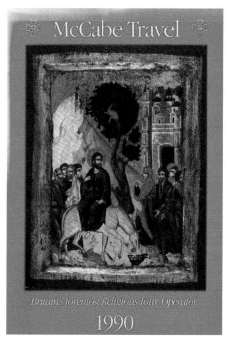

This poster from the Christian Resources Exhibition became a feature afterwards in our office, and was added to at a party by somebody adding the caption, "Pizza for Mr Iscariot"

Our First Financial Crisis   1991

McCabe was now recognised as a mainstream pilgrimage organiser, but five years of depressed travel to Israel and a financially unsuccessful Oberammergau season took their toll. We had built a business appreciated by many, but which was struggling to break even. We had no reserves and were living hand-to-mouth. There were two core financial problems: each year, the business was growing but the cost of running the company was increasing at the same rate. Our second problem was the fact that we had too much clients' money invested in property, so not immediately available in a time of need. As well as my house in Tooting, the company now owned my parents' and aunt's houses in Edinburgh and, in 1989, we took out a 125-year lease on larger office premises, including a residential flat. For this, we borrowed £250,000 over ten years, the logic being that we would eventually have an asset, rather than just pay rent.

This could have been a good strategy, building the capital base of the company through investment in property which would quadruple in value over the next twenty years. Unfortunately, we learned too late that this is a risky business strategy, especially in the unstable political arena we were working in. When we needed the cash, it wasn't easy to sell these assets and we came close to meltdown. Our lack of start-up capital, failure to make sufficient profit, and too much clients' money tied up in property almost brought the company down.

We did what we could to reduce costs including reducing staffing from seven to three. Ursula retired and Philip and Fiona moved on. Rosemary also left the company for what would prove to be a three-year break. I took a minimal salary and rented out my house, moving into a room above the office and Stuart contributed a generous loan, but there were still big question marks over our ability to survive.

Things came to a head at Easter 1991 when we were summoned to a meeting at Barclays bank and told that our bank loans had to be repaid within four weeks. A particular bone of contention was that we were not allowed to meet the decision makers. Nameless bankers had decided our business was not viable and our banking facilities were being withdrawn. For us to continue, Barclays wanted a significant injection of capital. My father and I were still the only directors, so I drove to Scotland, quite relaxed, accepting defeat.

My father asked me how much money would help, and my throw-away answer was that £50,000 would facilitate another week, £100,000 another month, but a realistic figure to give the company a chance – and only a chance – would be £200,000. George made a phone call and £200,000 was produced.

He died twelve months later on 6 May 1992, sadly only 66 years old, but not before he had secured the next thirty years of the company's future. The McCabe family had no financial reserves, but George knew someone who did. Revd Susan Cowell believed in us and lent the full amount for an indefinite period, interest free. It took nine years, but the loan was repaid in full, after a successful Oberammergau 2000 season.

Susan is pictured here with my mother and below with my parents in India. A school teacher and Elder of my father's church, Susan had a second career being ordained into the Church of Scotland ministry. She joined the Board of McCabe Pilgrimages for a time, as did my mother after my father's passing.

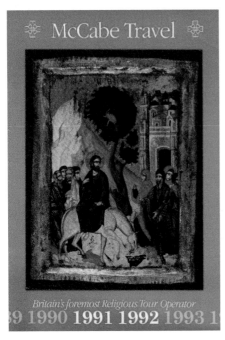

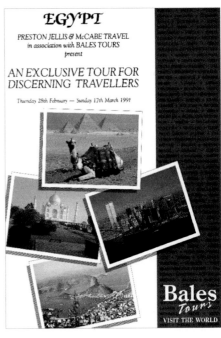

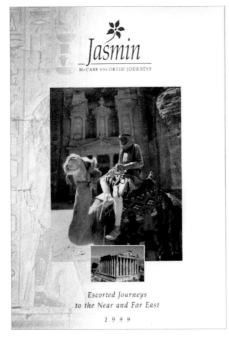

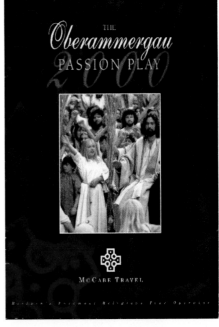

Our Golden Age

1992 - 2000

The next decade proved to be relatively crisis free with no wars or major unrest in the Middle East. We had survived our first financial crisis and for almost a year had kept the company going staffed only by myself, Robert, and Norma. In 1992, Norma returned to Ireland to marry and start a family. We were sad to see her go.

Mark Saunsbury, a local travel agent replaced Norma and became the anchor person around whom the office expanded. We recruited Andy Webster from our competitor, Orientours, and in 1993, Rosemary returned after a three-year break, with newly learned accountancy expertise. My sister Anne took a break from nursing and joined the team working remotely in Wilmslow. Staffing had doubled to six.

The business grew rapidly, thanks mainly to an expanding programme of Introductory Tours for potential tour leaders. Robert, Andy, Rosemary and Anne took turns accompanying these and we built relationships with new churches all over the country. Andy calculated that over the 27 years (and counting) of his time at McCabe he has accompanied more than a hundred parties. We had a growing reputation, and word of mouth was our main source of new business. We spent a lot of time on the road visiting tour leaders and conducting preparatory meetings. By the end of the decade, we would be a team of fifteen. Our excessive office space was filled!

Mark is pictured here with Moses Donaldson at our wedding, and below Andy and Anne with Margaret Jackson.

Being Part of a Thriving Pilgrimage Community

This was also a period of growth in our market generally. Competitors now included, in no particular order:

Worldwide Christian Travel, Tangney Tours, Fellowship Tours, Lionheart Tours, Highway Holidays, Star Tours, Vacanza, Peltours, Tyche, Special Pilgrimages, Longwood, Pax, Mancunia, St Peter's Tours, Jasmin, Bales, Maranatha, Israel Travel Service, Raymond Cook, Mastersun, as well as the original big two – Orientours and Inter Church Travel. As I write, of the 22 companies named here, only four including McCabe are still trading. Pictured is Rene Siva at our wedding. Rene was then manager of our arch rival Orientours but, like myself would develop his own pilgrimage company and became more friend than competitor.

I am reminded of the Biblical seven years of feast followed by seven years of famine. During this time of growth, we lived comfortably, but were not generating sufficient profit to build any significant reserves - a failing that would cost us dearly in the years ahead.

Rosemary and Andy with loyal McCabe supporters, Bishop Michael Lewis and Rev John Robinson.

A Memorable Red Sea Cruise Project

This was an innovative idea and could have been a great success. Erich Reich, Director of Thomas Cook Holidays when they purchased Inter Church Travel, left Cooks to purchase ICT's main rival, Orientours and to establish a new company called Classic Tours. He was a great innovator and not afraid to experiment with new ideas, including employing someone with no tour operating experience (Lynne Boraston, later to become Lynne McCabe).

McCabe's venture with Erich was a comedy of errors and failed, but we learned a lot and the project became an important milestone in the McCabe story. Erich's idea was sound - we would offer a one-week circular cruise in the Red Sea sailing from Aqaba in Jordan to Sharm El Sheik in the Sinai and on to Hurghada in Egypt. Three iconic day trips would be to Petra, St Catherine's Monastery and Luxor.

In 1991, I sat in a meeting in the Orientours' offices with the potential partners in the project. Three pilgrimage companies would jointly market the venture: McCabe, Special Pilgrimages and Orientours, and we were joined by Captain Dargan, owner of a fleet of Turkish gulets. His boats were busy in the summer months and this project offered him a winter season. These small traditional sailing boats had around eight cabins and could accommodate up to fifteen people. We would sail in flotilla, so numbers were not limited.

Emma Bodossian at Royal Jordanian was our flights partner and Aref of Arab Falcon in Jordan would handle the ground arrangements.

The product was launched as a new idea for our regular leaders. I remember being quite intimidated by the company I was keeping and assumed that Captain Dargan was on top of the sailing aspects. It turned out I was the only person in the room with first-hand experience of the volatile seas and winds in the Gulf of Aqaba having arranged previous scuba diving trips there. (On one adventure, I remember waking up in Sharm to find our encampment mostly blown way).

We successfully marketed the project and sold a series of cruises. All that remained was for the gulets to re-position from their summer location in Turkey, sail through the Suez Canal and moor in Aqaba, ready for our winter season. Aref awaited the boats' arrival. As the flotilla rounded the tip of the Sinai Peninsula, reality struck. Windows were smashed by the prevailing wind and heavy seas and, for the gulets, Sharm proved to be the end of the line. Captain Dargan pulled out and the boats returned to Turkey.

Despite this, Erich was determined to still go ahead with the press trip planned for the following week. Horrified at the prospect, Lynne's efforts to persuade him to cancel it fell on deaf ears. Not one of Erich's best ideas - a press trip to promote traditional Turkish sailing boats which didn't exist! So, against her better judgement, Lynne escorted a group of journalists to meet Aref in Egypt. Instead of the luxury yachts, the party sailed from Aqaba on the public ferry to the Sinai - a nightmare!

Our project now had no boats and I regretted not discussing the weather at our first meeting. I would have pulled out then, but Erich suggested we find new boats and I agreed to travel to Egypt to meet Lynne and Aref to pursue leads. This was never going to be successful. I recall one evening sitting on the deck of an ocean-going yacht in Hurghada, in the dark on my own, looking at the expansive deck space protected by a six-inch guard rail and imagining our typically elderly clientele sliding off the sloping deck. Inside, Aref was talking business with the group of wealthy young Greeks who owned the yachts – asking questions like 'how fast does this boat go?'

Pictured above, Lynne and Aref boarding the Sinai ferry and a fun Sinai taxi journey

67

Erich contracted the yachts. I pulled out and refunded our clients. The yachts never turned up in Aqaba. The gulets story did not end here. We would later team up with David Price Williams and his company, Temple World, to offer a series of pilgrimages 'Sailing in the Wake of St Paul' in coastal Turkey, which would be successful. The Red Sea itinerary has since been operated, but with a large cruise ship.

This story on its own is fun but is memorable for other reasons. This is where Lynne and I became a couple travelling in Egypt together – and the main reason I agreed to go. It cemented a lifetime friendship with Rene Siva, then Pilgrimage Manager at Orientours, and Issa Tahhan, owner of Special Pilgrimages. We would collaborate on future projects including joint Oberammergau programmes. Emma at Royal Jordanian became a loyal supporter of all things McCabe and a lifetime friend.

Andy Webster, a friend of Lynne's from university days, left Orientours and became part of the core McCabe team. Lynne started working at McCabe in 1998 and would become a valuable utility player sometimes working full-time and at other times juggling two or three days a week around childcare, and sometimes being paid and sometimes not! Lynne has a publishing and PR background and a key skill she brought to the office was the production of our brochures, which we created individually for every pilgrimage.

McCabe Educational Trust

The McCabe Educational Trust

1990 saw the establishment of the McCabe Educational Trust, initially with the dual aims of enabling young people to travel on an outward-bound expedition to the Sinai Desert, and of providing a Bible Lands Resource Centre for pilgrims and church leaders.

Our first Chair was the Bishop of Bath & Wells, The Rt Revd George Carey, who the following year, would be appointed Archbishop of Canterbury. The first administrator was David Praill, a Fellow of the Royal Geographical Society and formerly a course tutor at St George's College, Jerusalem. Our launch party, on 4 June 1991, was graciously hosted by Archbishop George at Lambeth Palace. Pictured here with George are founder Trustees, James Cronin, Iain Paton, Maureen Allchin and Andrew Mawson.

The McCabe Educational Trust is a registered charity and a Limited Company independent of McCabe Pilgrimages. It has its own Board of Directors and separately audited accounts. The administration is done on a voluntary basis by McCabe Travel staff and, in addition, McCabe Travel contributes the Trust's running costs, so that every penny donated is sent in full to the projects we support.

McCabe Pilgrimages and the McCabe Educational Trust have worked together for thirty years and, as I write, MET has now given over £4 million in grants to people in need we have met on our travels.

Our initial goals were very different to where the Trust is now. Project Sinai was the first Trust initiative. Led by Revd Andrew Mawson (now Lord Mawson of Bromley-by-Bow), we raised funds to take inner-city youngsters on a life changing adventure in the Sinai desert.

We started before the internet was invented, when it was difficult to find information about the Holy Land and pilgrimage in general. For our second project, , new Trustee, Canon Peter Nicholson created a Biblical Resource Centre with a lending library for tour leaders.

Project Sinai 1990 – 1997

Project Sinai was, I think, a unique initiative, taking youngsters living in challenging conditions on a one-week expedition into the Sinai desert, combining an adventure pilgrimage with a personal development programme. The young people were hosted by Bedouin nomads with few personal possessions, living in tents. By day the participants would walk and camel ride in a terrain and culture totally alien to their everyday experience and in the evening, they would gather around open fires to prepare food and share stories, sleeping under the vivid canopy of the desert stars. They kept a common diary which everyone was encouraged to contribute to, and we have these in our archive.

Project Sinai was led by Andrew and McCabe Pilgrimages' director, Robert Trimble. Andrew and Robert identified young people that they thought would benefit from the scheme and preparation meetings were held. Fund-raising was an integral part of the project and included in 1995 McCabe's first sponsored walk on a circuit around Hyde Park in London. The young people were helped with fund-raising ideas, and the McCabe Educational Trust raised the balance of funds required. Logistics were undertaken on a voluntary basis by McCabe staff.

In the Sinai, our partners were a Bedouin family experienced in desert trekking and every trip was quite different depending on the make-up of the group and the leadership. Excellent group leaders included Richard Charteris, then Bishop of London, David Praill, Robert, Andrew, and staff from the Bromley-by-Bow Centre.

One memorable expedition brought together equal numbers of homeless sellers of the newly conceived *Big Issue* magazine and wealthy young city bankers. The result was a cover story in the March 1997 magazine. What did we learn? One lesson was in our fundraising. Using pictures of a homeless person and their dog, we realised we would have raised more money if we had been fundraising to give the dog a better home. Sadly, true.

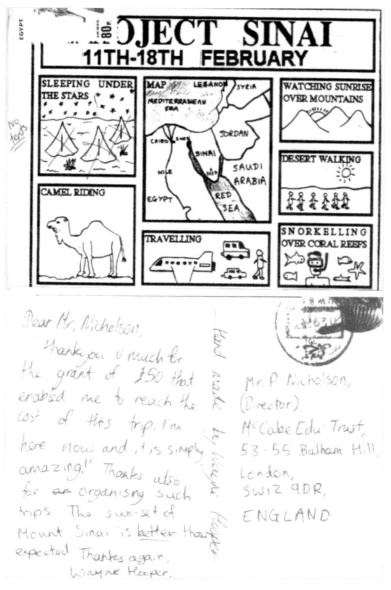

...OJECT SINAI
11TH-18TH FEBRUARY

SLEEPING UNDER THE STARS

MAP

WATCHING SUNRISE OVER MOUNTAINS

CAMEL RIDING

DESERT WALKING

TRAVELLING

SNORKELLING OVER CORAL REEFS

Dear Mr. Nicholson,

thankyou v much for the grant of £50 that enabled me to reach the cost of this trip. I'm here now and it is simply amazing!! Thanks also for an organising such trips. The sun-set of Mount Sinai is better than expected. Thanks again,

Wayne Hooper.

Mr. P Nicholson,
(Director)
McCabe Edu Trust,
53·55 Balham Hill,
London,
SW12 9DR,
ENGLAND

The Sinai was chosen for historical reasons: it has helped shape three of the world's great religions, but also so that the young people could experience the Bedouin way of life: no fixed abode and few personal possessions. Our goal was to expose them to a completely different culture, and to encourage them to think about their lives from a new perspective. We hoped that the experience would lead to higher self-esteem and give them hope and a vision of a life beyond their limited and largely negative daily routine.

Looking back, we provided an authentic desert adventure, unimaginably different from the young person's normal life experience.

Feedback from participants included Jamie, aged 22 'it has snapped me out of my unemployment weariness'.

From Rachel, aged 17, 'I'm sure this experience has helped me develop as a person and will stay with me for the rest of my life.'

And from Graeme, aged 17 'the most remarkable aspect of Sinai is the silence. In the desert there is an air of peace. It breeds clear thought, reflection, and trust'.

From John Evans, a retired headmaster and leader 'I have been on many educational trips in my career, but this was in a totally different class. The distinctive and unique feature was the combination of involvement and spiritual awakening among the young people. This seemed to grow naturally out of the desert itself'.

It is sad that the Sinai today is largely out of bounds for travel because of the threat from militant groups who have made this remote area their base. The Bedouin remain, and it is an ambition to return to this project in safer times and renew our partnership with these wonderful people.

Bible Lands Resource Centre

We are indebted to Canon Peter Nicholson who, on retiring as Director of St Luke's hospital for the clergy, in 1992 developed the flat above the McCabe office into a library and Pilgrimage Resource Centre. This was six years before Google and email culture was still ten years distant. (I found this lovely picture of Peter sitting proudly between George Carey and Robert Runcie, then current and previous Archbishop's of Canterbury)

Peter produced a monthly newsletter packed with news from the Holy Land, reviewed books and created a lending library of slide shows and other resources for pilgrimage preparatory meetings. When we started, there were only two helpful pilgrimage books, both written by regular Inter Church leaders. James Martin's *Plain Man in the Holy Land* is a day-by-day account of a typical pilgrimage, and Ron Brownrigg's *Come See the Place* was the definitive preparatory book for pilgrimage leaders. There was a big gap which Peter tried to fill.

We had a constant battle of minds with the Israel Government Tourist Office which would provide literature for us to distribute to pilgrims. I don't blame them, but much of it was propaganda that we were uncomfortable using. Gradually, we weaned ourselves off this easy and free supply of literature.

In partnership with Lion Publishing, a Holy Land Diary was published which we gave to every traveller. H J Richards produced the excellent *Pilgrim to the Holy Land*, and McCabe leaders, Norman Wareham and Jill Gill produced what would be the staple pilgrimage guide for the next thirty years, *Every Pilgrim's Guide to the Holy Land*. Instead of giving pilgrims a politicised free map from the tourist office, we partnered with a Jerusalem firm, and produced our own. The Christian Information Centre inside the Old City of Jerusalem offered personalised certificates of pilgrimage, which we presented to each pilgrim on the final night of their pilgrimage. These publications greatly improved the pilgrimage experience.

Our First Sponsored Walk

Fund-raising was an integral part of Project Sinai and included in 1995, McCabe's first Sponsored Walk in London's Hyde Park.

This was a lovely McCabe family day out in central London. We got agreement from the Royal Parks authority to set out a route in Hyde Park. Peter, Mark and a relaxed Andy can be seen here as marshals along the route. Robert brought his daughter along in a push-chair. Anne's family came down from Wilmslow, and Stuart from Scotland. A young Matthew can be seen here, very proud of his organiser's badge. The Bromley by Bow Centre played a big part in the organisation with many Project Sinai participants walking and raising funds for their trip.

Sunshine School

The McCabe Educational Trust has given the Sunshine School, a grant of £5,500 which will enable a fully equipped outdoor play area to be built.

The Sunshine School provides an excellent pre-school and early primary education in a Christian environment. The curriculum includes development of early-learning skills, art and crafts, drama, music and computer activities. Bible teaching and worship are central to the daily activities.

Marion's school is small, but the demand for Christian education is great. State education in Jerusalem is either Moslem or Jewish and all Christian establishments are privately run. We will keep in touch with Marion and try to help her as she expands her work in the Jerusalem Christian community.

The Sunshine School welcomes visitors and is encouraged by interest from Christians abroad. Write to Marion Jadon at POB 21699 Beit Hanina, Jerusalem or telephone Jerusalem 833825.

Canon Peter Nicholson visiting the Sunshine School.

The school is the vision of Marion Jadon, a member of St George's Cathedral in Jerusalem. Marion works on a voluntary basis and the school's future is dependent on school fees and outside help. We believe her work fits perfectly with the ethos of The McCabe Educational Trust, empowering people in their local situation.

"On behalf of the Sunshine School children, parents and staff I would like to thank you for your most generous gift of a playground. We have chosen the equipment and everyone is looking forward to the school being enriched in this way"

Marion Jadon

JERUSALEM CHRISTMAS GIFT

Initially an experiment, the Jerusalem Christmas Gift scheme has now been adopted as an integral part of the Trust's work. We are now collecting contributions for the 1997 Christmas Gift distribution. Last year we raised £4,000, an excellent result and our thanks go to the many churches and individuals who contributed. Walid Naber again supervised. "For the third year in a row", he reports, "the Christmas Gift distribution has been a success. Forty Christian families were helped in various ways; some with rent, some with school fees, some with a gift of essential supplies. I visited all of the families who were helped and they were all very appreciative."

CHILD SPONSORSHIP

Our child sponsorship scheme continues and the McCabe family now comprises six children in three countries. We receive regular letters from these young people whose opportunity in life comes from our reader's generous support. We will increase the number of young people we help as funds become available.

The McCabe Educational Trust Today

Today the emphasis has changed, and MET fundraises to support a variety of projects, with an emphasis on supporting Christian entrepreneurs we meet on our travels. Many work in difficult situations and they are encouraged by McCabe groups visiting their projects and by our financial support. The scale of our giving has increased and we are now able to give around £250,000 annually.

We have a guideline policy to give three quarters of available funds in structured regular support of three projects, with the other quarter being allocated at our Trustees' discretion. We try to keep £100,000 in reserve to protect our regular giving in a crisis – such as the recent Covid pandemic, when our reserves were called upon for the first time.

Another more recent initiative is to ask McCabe travellers to donate £15 to the Trust each time they travel and most do. We are grateful to loyal supporters who contribute monthly by Standing Order, and to those who have remembered the Trust in their will.

The company continues to cover the Trust's administrative costs, so that every penny of every donation, as has been the case since the Trust was formed, is given in full to the projects we support.

MET The Holy Land

Our principal projects in the Holy Land are the Jeel Al Amal Boys' Home in Bethany and the Al Shurooq School for the Blind in Bethlehem. We have been sending a quarterly donation to these projects for more than twenty years. Our support is not only financial, but group visits offer encouragement and build relationships, with many pilgrims spreading awareness and raising funds when they return home.

Every McCabe Holy Land pilgrimage itinerary includes a visit to either Jeel or Al Shurooq, so McCabe travellers have the opportunity to meet the staff and pupils. In addition, in Bethlehem, we provide income for the BASR Rehabilitation Centre when they host our groups for lunch. Pilgrims also purchase local Handicrafts here, adding to our financial support. The Director gives a talk about their work, and a relationship is formed. We have often been humbled by large individual donations from pilgrim visitors.

Our support of these projects works both ways, with pilgrims visiting coming away inspired by what they have seen. I believe these visits are the essential difference on a McCabe Holy Land pilgrimage itinerary.

Pictured above, Najwa, Director of Jeel al Amal. Helen Shehadeh, founder of Al Shurooq. MET trustee, Iain Paton with Helen's brother Edmund. A visit to Al Shurooq.

Former Archbishop of Canterbury, George Carey, was the first MET Chair and has given great support through the years. Here he is pictured with Edmund Shehadeh, Director of the Bethlehem Rehabilitation Centre.

A recent initiative by one leader is the setting up of a Scholarship Fund enabling Jeel al Amal children to attend further education. MET manages the fund and, from a fledgling idea, a reality emerges.

The Christian population of the Holy Land is rapidly disappearing, and we are proud of our small contribution to encourage them to stay. The scale of the social work done by a small number of Christian entrepreneurs is remarkable. All of the projects we support are under Christian Directorship but are staffed by Moslems and Christians working together and they all offer a remarkable caring service to all needy people in the community regardless of their religion.

They all also have another factor in common - they are totally dependent on voluntary assistance. It is our passion to give their work moral as well as financial support and the oxygen of publicity that MET gives has opened the door to many parallel sources of income.

'Our everyday life here is a miracle, in our work we sense the presence of Christ. God lives in this orphanage.'
Samar Sahhar, Jeel Al Amal Boys Home

Alice Sahhar, pictured above, was the entrepreneur, opening Jeel al Amal in 1972. Sadly, Alice died in 2008, but her daughters, Najwa and Samar continued the work.

MET India and Nepal

The McCabe family has a long association with India. My grandparents were missionaries for thirty years and my father and his brother Andrew followed in their footsteps. George spent eight years in the 1950s as farm manager of Dr Graham's Homes in Kalimpong, before becoming a Church of Scotland minister. Andrew died in 2017 at the age of 93, still serving in India, after a remarkable 67-year ministry.

Since it was founded, MET has supported Revd Andrew McCabe's work principally by making the Anand Niwas Boys' Home our third core project. This boys' home in a remote rural location near Lucknow, would typically look after a hundred needy boys at any one time and offer food, shelter, and schooling to what Andrew would describe as 'street kids'.

Andrew had a passion for helping children and firmly believed that the only difference between a well-dressed, articulate middle class child and a child living off his wits on the streets of one of India's big cities, was opportunity. As a family we are proud of the longevity of Andrew's ministry and the countless children given a life-changing start in life. His work was recognised when he was awarded an MBE in the 1992 Queen's Birthday Honours List.

In 1997 we helped to build a school in Nepal. Andrew identified the need. MET raised the funds and the Pahar Trust Nepal did the construction. The initial build cost £20,000 and, over the past 25 years under the supervision of MET trustees Bob Jackson and Roger Stoakley, we have developed the project, building a student hostel, installing a library, and introducing computers. Our partnership has been strengthened by Bob and Roger regularly escorting McCabe parties to visit the school as part of a wider India and Nepal itinerary.

We maintain the McCabe family connection with Dr Graham's Homes in Kalimpong, high in the Himalayan foothills. The school was founded by a Scottish missionary over a hundred years ago and maintains its strong Christian ethos, providing a first-class education and offering needy children an escape from poverty.

I was born here when my parents served as missionaries in the 1950s and it has been a privilege to take parties to North India and to visit the school. These visits have resulted in many McCabe travellers sponsoring children and MET is currently supporting five children through their education here.

MET is the 'heart and soul' of McCabe Pilgrimages, and I believe it is the Trust which sets us apart as more than just a travel company. It is this aspect of our work which has kept me emotionally involved in McCabe Pilgrimages for all these years. I am grateful to the loyal supporters who have served as trustees and formed an unofficial Advisory Board for McCabe Pilgrimages keeping us on the straight and narrow.

Pictured above are MET Trustee, Bob Jackson with two McCabe sponsored children, Jason and Anthony on a visit to Dr Graham's Homes. Andrew teaching a class in Dadhuwa. The new library MET installed at Dadhuwa school.

Andrew and the boys at the Anand Niwas Boys Home wearing hats donated by Margaretta Purtill. Below, my father talking to children on a visit to an Indian village.

Pahar Trust
Nepal

Helping to provide schools for the children
of the Nepalese Mountain Region

Thank you to

The McCabe Educational Trust

For the donation of   £ 22,047

Date   29th September 2012

PAHAR TRUST
NEPAL

The Politics of Holy Land Pilgrimage

We built on the legacy of Arthur Payton, and our hallmark became our support of the indigenous Christian community of the Holy Land. We have never seen ourselves as pro-Palestinian or anti-Israeli, but as Christians supporting Christians. Jerusalem is a city of Palestinian East and Israeli West and the general perception was that Palestinian standards were lower and East Jerusalem was potentially dangerous. We have never found either to be the case and we built an independently minded company with an East Jerusalem base.

We have watched the Christian community of the Holy Land become fewer and fewer, squeezed on the one side by the expanding Jewish state, and on the other by the predominant Muslim Palestinian community. Every year, many emigrate to find a better life for their families, mostly for economic reasons. As a company, we try to give them encouragement to stay, and keep alive this living link with the first disciples. We like to call the indigenous Christians 'the Living Stones' of the Holy Land. Sadly, the decline in numbers is dramatic. When we started, Bethlehem's population was more than 80% Christian; today it is less than 20%. In Jerusalem, the Christian population numbers less than 2% and the figure for the country is less. Those that remain are part of a committed community which plays a much larger part in society than their numbers would indicate.

We help economically by employing Christian guides and giving preference to Christian shops and restaurants. We admire the passion of the Christian entrepreneurs the McCabe Educational Trust supports and the way this Christian community shares a gospel of hope and serves those in need regardless of their religion. Every community in the Holy Land has its supporters and we have chosen to give our support to 'the Living Stones'.

As a business, we work across the political divide. Our principal airline is EL AL Israel Airlines. In Tiberias, our partner is the Jewish Amsalem family, owners of the Ron Beach Hotel. Our coaching is with the Arab Israeli Nazareth Transport Company, and in Jerusalem our McCabe base is the Palestinian Golden Walls Hotel. The Christian Albina family is 'McCabe in the Holy Land' and they look after all local logistics. It speaks volumes that these five partnerships have endured and strengthened over more than 35 years.

Local Guides Make a Pilgrimage

We work hard to prepare leaders and pilgrims for their visit and spend hours with tour leaders constructing itineraries built on each church's priorities. Arthur Payton only employed guides in the Jerusalem area, and groups would travel to the Galilee unaccompanied. Arthur's mantra was that the Bible was the only guide you needed. The driver knew the route, and the tour leader would bring the Bible to life in situ. A guide explaining dates and history was superfluous. This worked when tourism to Israel was in its infancy with easy traffic and un-crowded sites. We changed this policy, mostly for logistical reasons, and a guide now accompanies a McCabe group from airport back to airport.

Our choice of guides used to be very limited. In Jerusalem, there were a small number of, mostly Muslim Arab guides from pre-1967, when the Old City of Jerusalem was part of Jordan. Their knowledge was limited, and they were only allowed to guide in the Jerusalem area. The alternative was to employ Jewish guides. Some were excellent, but many had their own agenda and there would be a constant battle between the guide wanting to tell the story of the growth of modern Israel and our leaders trying to follow a carefully constructed pilgrimage narrative. Our battle was played out on a larger stage between the Vatican, represented by the Notre Dame Centre in Jerusalem, and the Israeli government.

Our guides: back row Dickran Torossian Walid Nabber (Albina office) Ibrahim Khoury Oliver Miller Saleem Musallam Ali Mir'i Ibrahim Jaber Adnam Shalabi Samer abu Hadeed. Front Row Shafik Khbeis Bassam Abdalla Rami Munayer Dahoud Manarious Alistair Rafi Tavittian Nasser Elias Anwar Khatib (Nazarene driver)

There was an impasse with the Israelis insisting that pilgrim groups be accompanied by an Israeli guide, and Notre Dame responding by saying that no Israeli guide would be allowed to enter a Roman Catholic owned Holy Place. An agreement was reached, that Notre Dame would issue 'green cards' to their clergy leaders, which would exempt them from the guide rule. Notre Dame expanded this exemption to other denominations and our experienced leaders were given cards. The Israeli guides were not happy and there was confrontation, especially at sites such as Masada and Caesarea where the guides rightly argued that these weren't pilgrim sites.

Our argument, and the Vatican's, was not anti-Israeli; it was making the point that our groups were on a pilgrimage to the Land of the Bible, and not tourists visiting modern Israel. We argued that a Jewish group touring Israel would rightly want to be guided by an Israeli Jew, and that a Christian party visiting Israel should have the option of being guided by a Christian. It took more than a decade for the status quo to change, but one of the agreements in the Oslo Accords was the 1998 opening of an English language guiding course at Jerusalem's Hebrew University, accessible to Arab students who either held an Israeli passport or Jerusalem ID card. Most importantly, graduates had the right to guide anywhere in Israel. For the first time, we could employ, young, enthusiastic and, most importantly, Christian guides to lead our pilgrimages. This was a huge breakthrough, and today we still work with many of that first batch of guides.

Leadership of a pilgrimage is shared between the group organiser and a local guide, and the balance is different on every pilgrimage. The guide will generally give a historical explanation with the spiritual leader then telling the Biblical story and conducting worship. Some leaders are happy for the guide to do most of the talking, while others will ask the guide to be brief. We emphasize the point that the group organiser is in charge. When groups return for a second or third pilgrimage, we try to provide the same guide and driver. This is not always easy to achieve as guides are freelance and choose which companies and groups they work for. For instance, guides weigh up the fact that Americans tip more than British pilgrims and like to shop more, but when trouble brews, American groups are the first to cancel. Guides prefer larger groups and many of our parish parties are small. McCabe has a reputation for playing fair, being organised and, importantly, for having appreciative travellers. It has not always been easy, but we have a loyal group of excellent guides who are the backbone of our company and a key McCabe strength.

Jasmin Tours

Jasmin 1997 Tours

EGYPT • ETHIOPIA • IRAN • ISRAEL
JORDAN • LEBANON • OMAN • SYRIA
EMIRATES • YEMEN

01628 531121

In 1997, we acquired Jasmin Tours, from my friend, Jim Smith, known in the travel industry as 'Mr Jordan' as Jim had been one of the ground breakers establishing the Hashemite Kingdom of Jordan as a holiday destination.

We attempted to do something outside of our comfort zone, offering non-religious small group escorted holidays to the Middle East, India, Nepal and even China. The acquisition was done with a handshake and, for continuity, Jim stayed with us for the first year and we recruited two dedicated Jasmin staff, Isabelle Marsan and Katy Leiper.

We paid a small purchase price for Jasmin but invested a substantial sum to try and revitalise the brand. We utilised an advertising agency and ran a national advertising campaign, and a specialist company distributed Jasmin brochures to travel agencies throughout the UK.

This was an expensive experiment, and we were competing with companies such as Bales Worldwide and Abercrombie & Kent who had much bigger promotional budgets. After three years, we cut our losses and dropped the brand name.

As with our Red Sea fiasco, the purchase of Jasmin was to bear fruit in many indirect ways. Jim introduced us to many of our current partners in the Middle East, not least the Albina family in Jerusalem and Ghada Najjar in Jordan, both still central to McCabe.

We were able to take Jim's carefully worked itineraries and expand the scope of our regular McCabe pilgrimages. Many churches were enthusiastic to travel further afield, and Iran, Egypt, Syria, Lebanon, and Libya were added to our destination list. We built on Jim's vast experience in Jordan with a portfolio of pilgrimages combining Israel with the Biblical sites on the Eastern side of the Jordan River. A very successful initiative was combining a week in Jordan with a sail across the Red Sea to St Catherine's monastery in the Sinai. Jim introduced us to his team of professional tour managers, who would become invaluable on our Oberammergau 2020 European coach programme.

I am very grateful to Jim for expanding our vision and bringing his wide-ranging travel experience to McCabe during what was to be our biggest growth spurt. The experiment also made me appreciate how fortunate we are to be operating as a major player in a small, loyal, niche market.

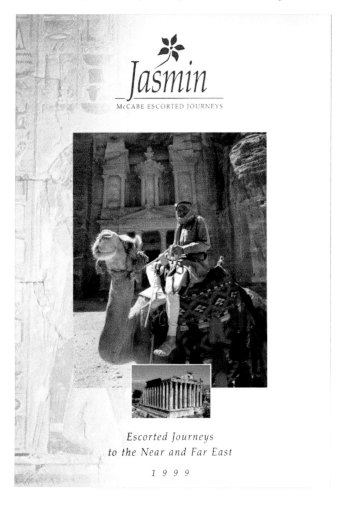

Escorted Journeys
to the Near and Far East

1 9 9 9

McCabe Partnership with BBC Religious Broadcasting

In 1995 we were selected to partner the BBC in the making of a Songs of Praise edition from the Holy Land. A choir of 150 people travelled and, in a busy 10 days, seven Daily Worship programmes and a Sunday Morning Service were broadcast live on Radio Four. Songs of Praise was broadcast on BBC One in the run up to Christmas.

Revd Stephen Shipley and Diane Reid produced, with Pam Rhodes presenting. McCabe made the travel arrangements for the choir and production crew as well as facilitating the various locations for worship and recording. Particularly memorable, was the filming of 'Dear Lord and Father of Mankind' on the Sea of Galilee. Three boats sailed together, creating evocative pictures of the choir and the lake. Sound recording with the choir divided on three boats wasn't practical, so it was interesting to watch the production technique of the recorded sound coming from the choir singing in the hotel bar, which had great acoustics. John Cousins was the only cameraman and it was fascinating to watch him work, achieving the effect of multiple cameras by hymns being sung multiple times as John changed the camera position. It was also fun to watch the tensions between the TV and radio production teams as they tried to reconcile their competing agendas in a very tight time schedule.

Under the title, 'what could possibly go wrong?' goes a Communion service being filmed on the Mount of Beatitudes when an innocuous light aircraft turned out to be a crop sprayer and we were directly under its flight path!

Central to the itinerary were meetings with the local Christian community, and a highlight was our visit to Bethlehem, where we were hosted by another BBC, in the form of the Bethlehem Bible College, and their choir featured on Songs of Praise. Bishara Awad, founder and director of the college, organised lunch and a market of local crafts, giving the party the opportunity to meet local Christians and purchase embroidery and olive wood artefacts made by the Christian community.

McCabe's Mark Saunsbury did a fantastic job setting up shop and administering remedies for sunstroke, dehydration, and the inevitable tummy upsets. Mark was in his element travelling with groups and was never happier than when, with a clipboard in hand, he would organise anything and anyone in range!

A year later, wearing a kilt, clipboard at the ready, he escorted the guests travelling from London to Lynne and Alistair's wedding in Scotland, and in 2000 he became 'Mr Oberammergau' looking after McCabe guests in the village for the twenty week season.

Jeremy Bowen, then senior BBC political correspondent in Jerusalem, addressed the party after dinner one evening. His theme was that in Middle East reporting, expect the unexpected. His talk was prescient, as a few weeks later Israel's Prime Minister, Yitzhak Rabin, was assassinated by a Jewish extremist just as a peace deal seemed very likely. In hindsight, this is probably the closest Israel, and the Palestinians came to agreement. I often think of that talk as, 25 years on, I listen to Jeremy reporting from Jerusalem with peace an elusive dream.

Stephen Shipley was to be instrumental in arranging a series of BBC choir tours in the following years with itineraries based on St Paul's missionary journeys through Turkey and Greece. A highlight was a visit to the Convent of St John the Forerunner on a mountaintop in central Greece. We broadcast Daily Service live from here and had wonderful fellowship with a vibrant community of sisters sharing a contemporary monastic life. We were able to contrast this experience with our visit the following day to the iconic Meteora monasteries which, though spectacular to look at, had a feeling of living in the past.

We enjoyed this period in our company's life enormously. Part of the fun was the planning when we would take the BBC crew on preparatory visits, checking out rehearsal and performance venues. I remember in Thessaloniki being confronted with a locked church, calling the number on a note written in Greek stuck to the church railings, to find I was calling a lady offering a different kind of service!

BBC Songs of Praise party 1995

The McCabe Team in 1996

Natasha	Arwa	Alistair,	Robert	Marianne	Stuart	Vehanoush	Mark	Rosemary
Albina	Mhadin	Mollie	(& Ailish)	Albina	Director	Albina	Saunsbury	Operations
Jerusalem	Jordan	& Anne	Albina	Director	Jerusalem	Albina	Office Manager	Manager
		Director	Jerusalem			Jerusalem		

Preston Jellis Travel Club

Looking back, certain larger-than-life characters became part of the McCabe family. Preston Jellis, a retired civil servant in Cambridge, had a select mailing list of around 120 people and he arranged three holidays every year for his travel club. His rule was that everybody on the list travelled at least once every two years or they were taken off the list. Two of the holidays would be in Britain or Europe and reasonably priced (and not our concern). The third would be expensive and, typically, would

be a year in the planning. Preston loved researching these holidays which he did meticulously. Preston also enjoyed lunch and Rosemary and I had many a memorable meal with him developing the latest project. Some of these itineraries would be adapted for a wider McCabe audience but most were very special one-offs.

A big regret was only actually travelling on one of these holidays. The exception was a round-the-world trip. Preston's wife took ill shortly before departure, and I agreed to deputise as leader. Our party of twenty flew to Los Angeles and spent a day at Disney World then continued via Sydney to New Zealand. A two-week luxury coach tour around the North and South Islands was followed by a journey home via Singapore. During a Jellis tour, the expectation was that guests would dine in best available restaurants, a la carte, with food and drinks included in the tour cost. Every tour also featured a no-expense-spared Gala Evening: in Singapore, a fleet of rickshaws delivered us to Raffles Hotel where Singapore Slings were enjoyed in the iconic Long Bar, lobsters were dined upon in the courtyard restaurant and the hotel chamber orchestra serenaded us from the balcony above – a truly memorable evening for us all.

One holiday, which was little more than a day trip, comprised a return flight to the Arctic Circle with a twelve hour stay featuring a 'Titanic style' excursion in small boats amongst icebergs. What made it so special? We chartered Concorde and, the destination being over water, meant that the plane was allowed to fly at its supersonic speed of 1,350 mph. With hindsight, we should have spent the profits and joined them!

On some ventures we partnered an expert in the field: for China, our partner was Voyage Jules Verne, the Jellis Nile Cruise was with Bales, an expedition to Antarctica was with the Royal Caribbean Cruise Line, and a coach tour through New England in the Fall was in partnership with Tauk Tours. On more familiar territory, Preston's tours to Israel, Jordan, Greece, Turkey, Oberammergau, India, and Nepal gave us and our partners the opportunity to produce the ultimate itinerary without the usual cost constraints.

Preston sadly passed away in 1998 after a short illness. The travel club stayed together for several years under the leadership of regular travellers, Shirley, and Norman Baker, before disbanding. We enjoyed the opportunity to use our imagination with these projects and it was a great privilege to work with Preston, Norman and Shirley and be part of an appreciative group of regular travellers.

On a smaller scale, intrepid group travel organiser Frances Brown, and her loyal band of followers, developed our expertise in Iran, with regular and varied itineraries. Frances also conducted our first forays into Yemen and Libya.

Growing With Our Group Organisers

Partnerships with the BBC, Preston Jellis, Jasmin, and Frances Brown were the icing on the cake. Our second decade was successful because of the trust put in us by parish group organisers. The loyal band of early leaders was now joined by a new intake, bringing fresh ideas, energy, and their followers. I want to give a flavour of the sort of leaders who joined us and what they brought to McCabe.

Bob Jackson added depth to our relationships overseas and broke new ground with his adventurous itineraries. A railway enthusiast, in Jordan we would charter a steam train on part of the old Hejaz route.

Bob would be in the cab getting to know the crew and even arranged for uniforms to be made for them. In Nepal, Bob made it his business to find out the needs at the McCabe supported Dadhuwa school and raise money to supply them. In India, Bob is still in contact with two of our original McCabe sponsored boys at Dr Graham's Homes (both are now almost thirty years old). He led our first trip to Machu Picchu in the Andes and to seldom visited Bhutan. Bob became chair of the McCabe Educational Trust and his daughter, Ruth, joined our staff for a time.

Geoffrey Marshall is in the mould of James Currie - you can sleep when you go home! His energy has challenged us to keep expanding the scope of our pilgrimages. There are very few McCabe destinations that Geoffrey has not taken a party to and you can guarantee that 25% extra will be added to each day's programme. Geoffrey is deputy chair of the Trust and produces our newsletters. Like Bob, his daughter Sarah, has also been a member of our staff.

Richard Askew was rector of Bath Abbey and, together with his wife Margaret (who he referred to as the managing director), took meticulous care of the preparations for 23 pilgrimages with us. The brochures Richard and Margaret prepared were infinitely better than anything we produced ourselves. We learned much from Richard and Margaret and gratefully acknowledge their influence in the development of McCabe's brochures.

Iain Paton, pictured her with Alice at Jeel al Amal, is a Church of Scotland contemporary of my father and has loyally supported McCabe, leading parish parties, educational tours, and Scottish national pilgrimages. Iain is also a founder Trustee and the longstanding Company Secretary of MET ensuring the Trust is run correctly.

Kevin Dunne keeps us on our toes to find flights from Newcastle airport! A challenge is for us to find regional flights to avoid Scottish and Northern groups the long trek to Heathrow airport. Kevin is also a long-standing MET Trustee, leads Educational Tours and was instrumental in starting our Short Breaks programme.

Frank Cooke, Baptist minister, and Director of the Purley & Andover Christian Trust was in a similar vein to Richard Askew. At the time, we could be frustrated by the endless re-writes and detail of Frank's itineraries, but this seeped into our mainstream thinking.

Maureen Allchin joined us as a schoolteacher, became ordained and was a founder Trustee of MET. We thank Maureen for being instrumental in introducing us to many clergy who became pilgrimage leaders.

Our Jasmin experience taught us how expensive it can be to recruit a new client. We are indebted to Maureen and leaders like her who spread the word and were the vital link in making McCabe Pilgrimages such a success story.

Our First Management Shake Up   1999

The year 2000 was to be the most successful in the company's history. In one year, we would quadruple our business.

Our millennium Pilgrim 2000 project to the Holy Land had 2,000 participants. In addition, 12,000 people travelled to Oberammergau, and we had our normal programme of holidays alongside.

Staff numbers had grown to fifteen. On a personal level, Lynne and I were married in 1996 and Angus was born on 15 May 1998. Robert had been with the company twelve years and was also now married and bringing up a family. Our daughter Eva was born on 1 February 2000 and the reality of that year with dad working seven days a week, was that she didn't really meet me until October, as periods when I was at home and she was awake, were rare.

McCabe had expanded, maybe too quickly, to fifteen staff and we weren't all pulling in the same direction. Robert had an excellent sales team, including my sister Anne Pears and Andy Webster. Anne worked remotely in Manchester, which never really worked because of logistics. Anne had remote access to the McCabe computer system, but in practice the link was unreliable and frustrating. Nowadays, remote working is easy, with efficient and cheap broadband connections. Anne would visit churches in the north of England, see our groups off at Manchester airport and join monthly team meetings in London.

Alexandra joined us for a year from Salzburg as the German speaker on our Oberammergau team.

The culture of the office changed with our larger staff. We had lots of team meetings, long agendas, and an increasing divergence in management style. Robert typically wore a suit, was very respectful of the church and was building solid relationships with clergy at all levels, and, typical of the time, had a PA Jackie Humphries (a friend from Earlsfield Baptist Church days) who produced correspondence from a dictaphone.

I typically dressed casually and focused on the quality of the product, often quoting Rev James Currie's advice 'Alistair, you have a responsibility to your clients to stay in business'. Staff management was becoming an issue. We had grown quickly with the year 2000 approaching when we would quadruple the number of people travelling with us. Robert had a conciliatory, forgiving approach to staff management, whereas I was a stickler for detail and didn't, for instance, easily accept lateness or inaccurate work.

For the first time, the company was stable financially, and we were on track to fully repay Susan's £200,000 loan from 1991. I was looking for a new challenge with a dream of running a hotel in the Highlands and the stage was set for change.

Robert and Jackie are pictured here with Bishop Riah and Archbishop Tutu in the build up to Pilgrim 2000.

A New Management Team

From the minutes of a board meeting held on 8 March 1999:

After a week of intense discussion and negotiation, Alistair has resigned from his position as managing director in favour of a different style of management proposed by Robert Trimble and Rosemary Nutt.

Alistair will remain as chairman and majority shareholder influencing the overall direction of the company through formal monthly meetings with the new management team. He will continue managing the Millennium Oberammergau programme and leave the company in October 2000.

Robert steps up to become managing director. Rosemary is appointed director in charge of travel operations and Andy Webster becomes tours manager.

The result is a shuffle of existing directors and promotion from within the company to install an enthusiastic management team for our big Millennium year and with fresh ideas to take the company forwards. We have achieved something that few family-owned and operated companies accomplish: a smooth transition to new management, meeting the immediate needs of all concerned.

Weekly directors' meetings will be held between Rosemary and Robert, with contributions from key staff as necessary. Alistair will chair monthly meetings, monitoring targets and areas of concern, but will only get involved in major decisions affecting the company's future, or where there is no clear consensus in the management team.

The next eighteen months will be the busiest in the company's history, and these changes we feel are necessary for the company to go forward with everyone pulling in the same direction.

The management view, past and present is optimistic.

Rosemary was offered the top job but preferred to stay one step back supporting Robert.

Partnering Anglican Diocesan Pilgrimages

McCabe built relationships with Anglican dioceses and cathedrals up and down the country. Pilgrimages would sometimes number up to 150 people travelling under the leadership of the Bishop and supporting clergy. Some cathedrals like St Albans and Southwark (pictured here with Bishop Christopher Chessun and Dean Andrew Nunn) made pilgrimage an integral part of the life of the diocese with a team planning pilgrimages two or three years ahead. It was a privilege for us to become a part in the life of the cathedral and participate in planning and preparatory meetings.

Robert, Rosemary and Andy would travel with these parties handling the complex logistics of two or three coaches touring together.

The high point of this partnership was our Millennium project, when, under Robert Trimble's direction, we arranged 24 multi-coach pilgrimages to the Holy Land including national pilgrimages from Scotland and Wales, denominational pilgrimages from the Methodist and United Reformed Church, and twenty diocesan pilgrimages led by their Bishops.

The Millennium   Pilgrim 2000

'With all the hype that surrounds the Millennium, we are in danger of ignoring the simple central fact, that what we are actually celebrating is the birth of Jesus Christ' wrote Christopher Herbert, Bishop of St Albans, introducing the McCabe Millennium Project. 'Pilgrim 2000 offers a pilgrimage with a difference because pilgrims will also be visiting the local church in the Holy Land and supporting its work by raising money for specific projects. These gifts will be a thank you to the whole of Israel and Palestine for being the setting for the birth of Jesus and a sign of our fellowship with Christians living there today'.

Pilgrim 2000 was an attempt to revitalise the relationship between pilgrim parties and the indigenous church, encouraging pilgrims to build real relationships with 'the Living Stones' of the Holy Land. The project was a response to a challenge from Riah Abu El Assal, Anglican Bishop of Jerusalem, who wrote, 'in the new Millennium we want people to visit us. It is a wonderful experience to walk where Jesus walked, but it is an even more wonderful experience to walk with whom Jesus walked'.

A quote from Robert Trimble, who led the project for McCabe: 'our hope is that Pilgrim 2000 will transform the way that Christians view the Holy Land. Pilgrim 2000 allows UK Christians to not only visit that place, but also stand alongside our brothers and sisters living in the land of Jesus today' or, as Bishop Riah put it, 'Pilgrim 2000 will be a new kind of pilgrimage, focusing on people becoming partners for peace with us'.

McCabe arranged 24 major pilgrimages with 2000 pilgrims participating and together, we raised half a million pounds for projects run by the Christian community in the Holy Land.

Each party twinned with a specific project and these projects featured strongly in preparatory meetings, raising the profile of the ever-reducing Christian community in the Holy Land. Visiting the partner project was the highlight of each pilgrimage and afterwards the connection was maintained. The McCabe Educational Trust today makes it easy for partners in the UK to continue to give financial support to some remarkable projects given their moment in the sun by Pilgrim 2000.

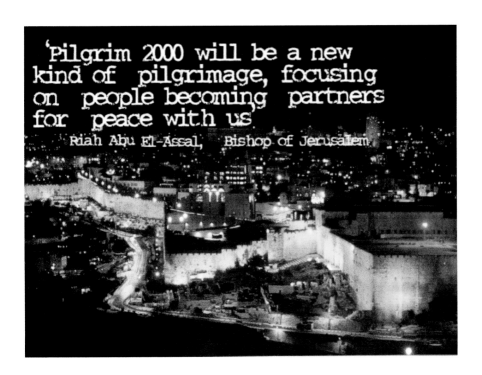

'Pilgrim 2000 will be a new kind of pilgrimage, focusing on people becoming partners for peace with us'
Riah Abu El-Assal, Bishop of Jerusalem

Oberammergau 2000

Planning for an Oberammergau season begins three years in advance starting with two financial challenges. We aren't paid for our work until after we successfully operate a holiday, so the budget for the three preparatory years must be covered in advance, and secondly the Civil Aviation Authority (CAA) insists on the company having a large amount of capital in the company before the season starts. For 2000 our target figure was, for us, an almost unachievable £500,000.

Adding to the financial pressure, the Oberammergau Village Council requires full payment for tickets six months before performances begin and we signed a charter flight contract with Airtours requiring a large deposit.

From a risk assessment point of view, much that could possibly go wrong in an Oberammergau season has gone wrong at some point during the four seasons in which we have participated. The 1990 ticket scandal was followed by charter flight problems right through the Millennium season. Then, the financial crash of 2008 added £2 million to the cost of our 2010 holidays. Also in 2010, the Icelandic volcano ash cloud closed most European airports for the opening weeks of the season. To cap these, in 2020 the world was under lockdown with the Covid-19 pandemic and, just two months before the first performance, the whole season was postponed for two years.

2000 was to be our most successful Oberammergau season, with a first class McCabe team delivering a fully booked season of excellent holidays. Panorama Tours in Salzburg became our local partner with Sybille Schauderna, Werner Bischof and Erica Fuchshofer, the key players. This would be my

second Oberammergau season with Sybille. I was most impressed at our first meeting in Salzburg when Werner produced Maria von Trapp's accordion from his cupboard!

Mark Saunsbury moved from the London office to Oberammergau and became a much-loved personality in the village. Airport meet and greet was arranged in co-operation with Christian Hoechner, an Oberammergau resident steeped in the play, and the Revd Michael Counsell took charge of the Ecumenical Centre and our teams of rotating vicars.

New Oberammergau Initiatives

For the 2000 season, we accepted accommodation in Oberammergau village for one-night stays, as well as two nights, increasing the number of people we could take to see the play. We also ventured away from Salzburg, accommodating groups in the Austrian Tyrol. Being less than two hours' drive from Oberammergau, made it easy for guests to attend a performance in the middle of their holiday. Werner introduced us to the Zum Hirschen and Arzlerhof hotels owned by the Staggl family, and the Inntalerhof Hotel owned by Daniela Heidkamp and these hotels would become solid McCabe partners for three Oberammergau seasons.

Our initiative was to book Tyrol hotel rooms for the full seven nights so that guests would not need to vacate their rooms when they travelled to Oberammergau for their overnight stay. They would travel the day before the play, enjoy time in the village and attend the evening event at the Ecumenical Centre. The following day, after the play they would return to the Tyrol for dinner and then had the remaining days of their holiday to share their Oberammergau experience.

Coach Tours to Oberammergau

Our 2000 coach programme was designed by two professional guides that I met on a Nile cruise: Carmen Wadel and Jeanne Roese planned the programme and introduced us to a Southampton coach firm who purchased three new coaches for our contract. These coaches came out of the factory dressed in McCabe colours with 'McCabe to Oberammergau' written on the side. We collected groups from pick-up points near their home church and twelve days later, dropped them back again. Logistically, this was sometimes a challenge, with the coach dropping a group off in Edinburgh and then picking up the next group in Cardiff but the season is still a much-talked-about success.

Central to our European itinerary was contracting the Xander, a first-class hotel in a wonderful rural location in Austria's Leutasch Valley. Some coach parties would stay here for three nights before spending two nights in nearby Oberammergau, while other coach parties would go to Oberammergau first for one night then spend four nights relaxing at the hotel. So, we filled the hotel for the whole season. We rented an apartment beside the hotel for our drivers, and this became a home-from-home for them and an official break from driving, enabling them to do quick turnarounds back in the UK. We also had facilities here to wash and clean the coaches and access to the garage of our local coach partner for maintenance.

English parties would cross the channel at Dover with guided visits to Bruges, Roman Trier, Ulm Cathedral and a sail on the Mosel River en route to Leutasch and Oberammergau. On the return journey, we visited Innsbruck and Colmar, with a last overnight at Reims, before crossing the channel. Our Scottish parties took an overnight ferry from Hull to Zeebrugge joining the route at Bruges. We were blessed with an excellent team of tour managers led by Jeanne and Carmen and including tour managers from our Jasmin era.

Pictured overleaf are Alexandra, who spent the season in the McCabe London office, Sybille, Erica Fuchshofer and Werner Bischof.

The Charter Flight Seemed Like a Good Idea!

Our original plan was to charter two aircraft, flying from Manchester and London to Salzburg. The problem we were struggling with was flight times, with most schedules requiring either a very early departure or a late return. We found a solution: Airtours, based in Manchester, had a very large standby aircraft. They agreed to charter this McDonnell Douglas DC10 with 366 seats to us every Tuesday. The plane would depart Manchester at 10 am, pick-up at Stansted at 11 am arriving Salzburg early afternoon. With a quick turnaround, travellers arrived home early evening. Ideal.

This is still the biggest plane to fly into Salzburg airport. The co-operation on arrival was fantastic. We had seven parties on board, heading to different hotels. Luggage was colour-coded and transferred directly from the plane to waiting coaches and passengers were received with minimal passport formalities. We had a team giving wheelchair assistance, and coaches would depart within an hour of touchdown. On the other side of the airport, departing travellers were checked in quickly at multiple desks, and the plane would depart, full, within 90 minutes.

Irritations included the crew trying to serve a hot meal in too short a time. Bizarrely, looking back they wanted us to pay extra for a cold meal. Nowadays, even British Airways only offers a sandwich on such a short flight. Positives included showing a charity appeal film en route and collecting loose change for The Roy Castle Foundation.

Our biggest challenge was the plane's reliability. The season was plagued with technical faults which caused shorter and longer delays. There was a repeated problem with a cargo door not locking securely. Our nightmare scenario happened on 15 August when, after a lengthy delay, the problem was not resolved. In this situation, the airline is responsible, but solutions can be slow to be put in place. We had staff at Manchester airport, and Rosemary and I took charge in London. A new aircraft was sourced, but our Stansted departure had to be changed to Gatwick. Rosemary arranged four coaches to transfer 200 tired and upset passengers. Our next problem was that Salzburg airport has a night curfew and the departure time from Gatwick was becoming critical. We made the decision to leave baggage at Gatwick, and the plane departed with a very tight window to beat the curfew.

In Salzburg, Werner was in the control tower cajoling flexibility from Salzburg air traffic control. The plane landed and passengers disembarked off the rear of the plane, while passengers boarded at the front. With a little leeway from Salzburg flight control, the plane departed forty minutes after touch-down, flew to Manchester first and then on to Stansted. Rosemary and I were leaving Gatwick airport in the early hours and saw the plane arrive empty back at base - mission accomplished. Baggage was delivered the next day. If the plane had not been allowed to land in Salzburg, 366 people would have returned to Rosemary and I at Gatwick, and Werner and Sybille at Salzburg airport would have had to find accommodation for the 366 departing passengers - a very close call and a date that none involved will forget.

Living and Working in Oberammergau Village

It is a privilege to live and work in the village of Oberammergau while the performances are taking place and McCabe is one of the few companies who set up an office in the village. We have built a reputation for going the extra mile to look after our travellers, and locally we are appreciated for bringing people who are knowledgeable about the history of the play and interested in the villagers' lives. Pictured here is Anton Preisinger. His grandfather played Jesus in 1950 and 1960. His father played Pilate and Tony will play the same role in 2022.

The season is long and hard for all involved, with 4,500 people arriving and departing five times a week over twenty weeks. There are no quiet weeks with the season fully subscribed. We meet and greet every arriving group, inviting them to the evening's event at the Ecumenical Centre. On play day mornings, we visit the guest houses, answer questions, and replace lost tickets. In the interval and after the play, our chaplains are available to chat. It is a relentless round of baggage handling, especially to the less accessible houses in narrow streets. Between departures and arrivals, we visit the Guest Houses with details of the next arriving guests. We gain brownie points by letting the owners know when their people will arrive so that they can gain a few hours, where other hosts needed to be on hand for arrivals at any time. In 2000, we were allocated all the rooms in Gasthof Zum Stern in the village centre, and this became our staff canteen and McCabe base in the village, with proprietor Johanna Lang an honorary member of our team.

When the people are in the play, the village is suddenly quiet, and our representatives have time to do their washing, go for a swim in the excellent swimming complex or just catch up on sleep. A fun thing to do is to sit outside the theatre and watch the comings and goings. The village children, for instance, all take part in the play's biggest scene, a re-enactment of Palm Sunday. Waving palm branches and shouting 'Hosanna', they surround Jesus as he makes his triumphal entry into Jerusalem riding a donkey. Dressing room space backstage is at a premium, so teachers dress the children at school and a procession of bikes heads towards the theatre and, after their big moment, its back to school again.

Mid-July, the halfway point in the season, is marked with parties and in September a weariness creeps in as the end is in sight. Our remedy to this is to give the London staff the opportunity to live in the village, bringing new energy to the final weeks of the season.

The Last Performance

At the end of the season, the last performance is reserved for a local audience and is an emotional event. The villagers have kept their vow, have worked hard and the energy on stage and in the audience is palpable. As the play nears the end, the doors are opened to reveal a theatre surrounded by villagers there to witness encores and final curtain calls. The village party afterwards has a hairdressing theme, as the players lose their long hair and beards amongst much jollification.

For our staff, it's an evening and a season they will never forget.

Our own end-of-season party with our partners in the village involved driving to Lucerne for a very special weekend. Memories include two-year-old Angus not coping with earache on the mountain cable car, a party on the lake with our chartered boat going round in circles, and a karaoke dinner with Mark singing *My Way* which summed up his approach to Oberammergau teamwork!

Parties followed in Salzburg and Strobl with hoteliers, local reps, guides, and drivers, bringing home what a unique experience being part of an Oberammergau season is.

Reflections on the Company in Millennium Year

Looking back, I regard the Oberammergau 2000 season as the peak of McCabe. I started the company when I was 30 and by 47 had achieved most of my ambitions. I tried to leave at this point but fate intervened and I would retire twenty years later at the age of 67. The energy buzzing through those first seventeen years was exciting. Being youngish and building a young team was part of it, being single was also a part of it. For most of this time the company teetered on the brink financially, but I could live cheaply and had no family responsibilities.

I travelled enjoyed travelling extensively. Particularly memorable were invitations from Emma Bodossian at Royal Jordanian Airlines to visit Jordan with competitors who would become lifelong friends. Similarly, Tim Gallagher (pictured here) at EL AL would invite us on trips to Galilee, still one of my favourite places. Many people commented on the fact that the pilgrimage organisers were friends first and competitors second, and we would help each other whenever we could.

These trips were much looked forward to and were a great opportunity to let our hair down with a group of people who liked and trusted each other and shared the same problems. We also travelled together to the Negev Desert, Syria, on a Nile Cruise and sailed on gulets in Turkey. These trips were educational but appreciated mostly for the opportunity for good friends to travel and spend time together.

Until the mid-1990s, the travel industry was an incredibly social one. Salaries were low, but this was made up for by the perks. We were routinely offered airline seats and holidays at a fraction of the normal price.

I love this relaxed picture of Ghada, our Jordanian partner, pictured on the beach in Aqaba with Emma (Royal Jordanian) and Nick Oliver (Lionheart Tours) behind her.

I took advantage of a 90% discount on a two-week Caribbean cruise, and memorably travelled all around India on one open-ended 75% discounted ticket. This was an era of long lunches and, looking back, I wonder when the work was done. One answer is that in these pre-internet days, there were many more staff than typically there are now.

Every airline had a group of 'reps' with a budget to wine and dine tour operators like us. This era came to an end in the late 1990s when the internet changed the travel world. First to go were the airline reps, who became redundant in a world where travel decisions were now made on computer screens. With the demise of the reps, went the budget for the long lunches. The internet meant people expected answers quickly, so lunch breaks in general largely disappeared. The internet enabled the emergence of Ryanair and EasyJet with a new business model of selling tickets with daily changing prices. The era of the £10 ticket had arrived. The rest of the industry followed suit, and 'special' bargains for travel staff ended. Our much-loved educational trips became fewer as airlines became more sophisticated in their promotional activities. Life in general in the travel industry was a lot less fun.

The first naïve years of McCabe were behind us and, by the autumn of 2000, for the first time we were financially stable. We repaid Susan Cowell's £200,000 loan. The company was now a well-respected leader in our pilgrimage world. Led by Robert, Rosemary, Andy and myself, our expertise was unrivalled, and we were on track to become the biggest UK pilgrimage operator. My plan had been to leave the company after Oberammergau 2000 but retain my shareholding. Politics intervened and this didn't happen. The following twenty years of married life would be very different from what Lynne and I had planned. For the next decade, work and our home life would become dominated by financial survival.

Above is a favourite picture with Rene Siva (then Tyche Tours) and Emma on a visit to Wadi Rum.

118

Survival

A Decade of Political and Financial Turmoil

2001 - 2010

The Second Intifada 2000 - 2006

If we'd had a crystal ball, we would have seen the Millennium heralding six years of unrest in Israel and the Middle East, and the second near total collapse of the business. Our financial salvation was all in the timing. Both Pilgrim 2000 and Oberammergau 2000 were mostly completed before disaster struck. The next decade was to be our most challenging, with hardly a stable moment in ten years.

The second Intifada began on 28 September 2000 and was different from the first, when the Palestinian resistance had focused on civil disobedience and stone throwing. This time, Hamas were to the fore and employed the terrifying weapon of suicide bombers. Sadly, more than 3,000 Palestinians and 1,000 Israelis would lose their lives during five years of conflict. It was clear that the risk to visitors was too great and, along with most travel companies, we cancelled our pilgrimages.

Most Middle East crises are short-lived, and we had become accustomed to business interruptions so, when the Intifada started, we thought in terms of maybe a maximum three-month business interruption. If we had known then that we would have no Middle East business for five years, I am not sure we would have carried on. After five years without a Holy Land pilgrimage, we emerged as quite a different company.

On 11 September 2001, re-enforcing our no travel decision, the Twin Towers in New York were brought down by Al-Qaeda leading to the second Gulf War (The Iraq War) in March 2003. This period in the company's history exemplifies the underlying uncertainty of a business operating in an unstable political environment. In the five years building up to the Millennium, the number of McCabe travellers had trebled and, with solid advance booking for 2001 and 2002, we anticipated continued growth.

I was stepping down, a new management structure was in place, and we planned to keep most of our staff on board. We could see clearly where the company was heading and, for the first time, we had financial reserves. But working with the Middle East, life can change quickly. With the new intifada, our rapid expansion was halted, and the new management structure reversed. We cancelled 270 groups booked to travel in 2001 and refunded more than 5,000 travellers. We were now in survival mode and big decisions had to be made quickly.

We reduced our overheads by moving to smaller premises, close by for continuity, so that we could keep the same phone number and post could easily be redirected. We closed Jasmin Tours.

Robert's period as managing director was to last less than two years, with me returning to the position for the next twenty. Robert had done sterling work with us for fourteen years and was quickly head-hunted to become director of the Bromley-by-Bow Centre, a post which, as I write, he still holds. Rosemary and I kept the ship afloat for five difficult years assisted by Joan Trimble (Robert's sister-in-law) who was the bedrock of the office juggling work and the school run, and Andy, who rose to the challenge and became the main link with our leaders.

We began 2001 with fifteen staff and ended the year with four: myself, Rosemary, Andy and Joan.

We diversified. An option not available to our partners in the Holy Land. At the Golden Walls, Fahmi used the time to redecorate and make general repairs, with waiters and cooks up and down ladders, but this was a disastrous time for hoteliers, restaurateurs, guides, drivers, shop owners and the Albina family, our partner office in Jerusalem, who could only wait for the crisis to end. We helped where we could, for example, lending money to Fahmi to help fund the renovation, and I remember we contributed to the cost of the bedding being changed from blankets to duvets. These acts of solidarity were greatly appreciated and would strengthen our core relationships when business returned.

Developing New European Itineraries

We responded by developing new itineraries. Churches that couldn't now travel to the Holy Land were offered alternative destinations. Rosemary and I travelled widely developing new itineraries in Spain, Turkey and Italy. The Church of England Wives Fellowship was our first party to travel on *The Camino* where we introduced an innovative ten day itinerary covering the 460 miles from Roncesvalles on the French Spanish border to Santiago de Compostela. We travelled by coach and each day combined a two or three hour walk on 'The Way' with visits to cathedrals, monasteries, and pilgrim chapels.

In Turkey, we teamed up with David Price-Williams who owned a fleet of the traditional sailing boats that we tried to use unsuccessfully in the Red Sea. David, an accomplished academic, conducted cruises exploring the archaeological sites on the Turkish coast. Together we developed one-week cruises 'Sailing in the Wake of St Paul' incorporating sections of his missionary journeys, with the extensive ruins of Ephesus being a highlight. These pilgrimages were totally different to anything we had done before and were great fun.

Each gulet had seven or eight cabins and we would sail in flotilla along a wonderfully unspoilt coastline, anchoring for the night in a sheltered bay or mooring in a small port. David is a great raconteur and would sometimes accompany a party and enthral with after dinner talks when we would all gather for drinks on one boat. To offer varied itineraries we combined land-based tours including 'The Seven Churches of Revelation' or the rock churches of Cappadocia with a shorter cruise. Sadly, we no longer offer these holidays, as the cost of the gulets kept increasing beyond the reach of a typical McCabe traveller.

In Italy, our big discovery was the unassuming family run Garden Hotel in the Umbrian village of Citta Di Castello. I remember walking through this very ordinary village with Rosemary, looking for an interesting restaurant for the evening, and not finding one.

We ate at the Garden Hotel and discovered it was the place to eat in the village! The rooms were small, but it had a nice garden and pool and excellent restaurant. We had chosen the village for its location. Our itinerary combined five days in Rome with five days at the Garden Hotel which, like spokes of a wheel, was within day trip distance of Assisi of St Francis, medieval San Gimignano, Siena and Florence.

Thirty European tours in 2002, peaked at seventy in 2005 as the Intifada finally came to an end. Since those days we have always tried to keep a balance in the company between Middle East and non-Middle East tours. A policy which worked well until the pandemic of 2020 stopped all travel everywhere!

Looking back, Lynne regards this period as the company at its best. I was in my forties, with Rosemary and Andy ten years younger. We were forced to almost start the company again, but this time from a solid base of loyal customers and with a financial cushion from our millennial year.

A different pattern of working emerged. I would make plans for the year ahead, and Rosemary would oversee the current year (I often wrote the wrong year on cheques!) We also co-operated to take a proper holiday break, Rosemary taking July off, followed by me taking August – and we would have no contact with the office while we were away, a rare period of work life balance. This pattern continued when business returned.

Computer technology was developing fast, and we invested in upgrading our tour operating system which meant we could grow with fewer employees. When business returned, we quickly rebuilt to the previous numbers of travellers, but with half the staff. What Lynne had noticed and commented on was that we had become a lean, efficient business with a happy atmosphere. The three of us knew what we were doing and were happy putting in the long hours with the invaluable part-time support of Joan.

Restoring Staff Levels After The Intifada

Alistair, Rosemary, Letty, Nada and Lynne with our carriage driver
in Salzburg on a staff winter break.

When business did return in 2006, we increased our staff to eight, half
of our 2000 peak, and we have kept to roughly that number since,
which has been a key factor in keeping the company profitable.

We recruited Letty Butler – in Nazareth. I had a call from Razi, manager
of our partner Nazareth Coach Company, saying that Letty who was
married to the son of one of the company owners, was returning to
England and was looking for employment. Letty joined us and gave us
ten years of loyal service, taking charge of our new reservation system
as well as contributing in very many other ways.

A year later, in similar circumstances, Nada Nashashibi, daughter of
the owner of the Golden Walls Hotel, married and moved to London.
She too would be part of our family for the next decade. Nada had
qualified as a Graphic Designer and for the first time we had someone
professional looking after our brochure design.

Both Nada and Letty took a big interest in the McCabe Educational
Trust, which from the beginning has been managed on a voluntary
basis by staff members.

Matthew pictured with Alison and Rachel in Oberammergau.

My nephew, Matthew Pears joined us straight from university to work with me on the upcoming Oberammergau season, but we were also aware of a possible succession strategy within the family. Matthew spent the summer of 2010 in Oberammergau as a key member of our team in the village.

We recruited Rachel Simpson to take charge of our Oberammergau flight programme. Rachel has a background of working in major travel companies, and this was the first time that we specifically recruited a travel professional. Today, Rachel is an established member of the McCabe team and is putting in place a flight programme for the delayed Oberammergau 2022 season.

Completing our Oberammergau team, we recruited Alison Mah and Katarina Plancha (pictured here with Nada) and with the children now a little older, Lynne spent more time in the office, covering holidays and illness.

Add Andy, and we had a talented new team to take the company forwards.

Our 20ᵗʰ and 25ᵗʰ Anniversaries in Oberammergau

In 2003, during this difficult period of unrest, 330 loyal supporters joined us as we celebrated McCabe's 20th anniversary with a memorable week in Austria and Oberammergau, where we attended a performance of *Nabucco* in the Passion Play Theatre. The Slaves Chorus, performed on an open-air stage with the Passion Play choir arranged around open fires, was breath-taking. We filled the parish church for our Anniversary Service, our joyful singing making a lasting impression on a village used to a more solemn style of worship.

For the second part of the holiday, we divided, with Lynne and I hosting a gala dinner at the Inntalerhof Hotel in the Tyrol (with Angus and Eva asleep under the table), and in Salzburg, Rosemary and Anne hosting a night of opera and inspiring speeches at the historic Mozart Dinner Concert venue of St Peter's Monastery. We repeated this idea in 2008, celebrating our 25th anniversary with a long weekend in Oberammergau village, this time attending an equally memorable performance of St Matthew's Passion. Our gala dinner this time was held in a village hotel.

These two events helped us through difficult years, but also built our reputation in Oberammergau prior to our application for tickets for the 2010 Passion Play season. The system in the village was to give priority to companies that supported the village during the quiet years between performance seasons.

Conflicts in Gaza

In the summer of 2005, the Intifada ended and Holy Land pilgrimages started again with fourteen parish groups travelling that autumn. But the next conflict was already on the horizon. In January 2006, Hamas unexpectedly won the Palestinian General Election. The always tense Gaza-Israel border became a war zone with rocket attacks on Israel from Gaza and retaliatory attacks by Israel. Having just re-started our Holy Land pilgrimages, we cancelled most of our 2006 season. The peak of hostilities would come in 2008 with sadly more than 1,000 people losing their lives in this three-year period. Remarkably, during 2007 and 2008, our pilgrimages continued as the conflict was not affecting most of Israel, and the company gradually returned to stability with more than half of our pilgrimages again being to the Holy Land.

Global Financial Crisis

We moved from political crises smoothly into a financial one. On 15 September 2008, the investment bank Lehman Brothers collapsed, sending shockwaves through the global financial system. The British banking system only survived with the government taking large stakes in amongst other banks, Northern Rock and the Royal Bank of Scotland. We worked through the deepest world recession since the 1920s with unemployment soaring. The biggest impact on us was the British Pound losing 25% of its value. We buy foreign currency to pay our overseas suppliers and the increased currency cost on a typical Holy Land pilgrimage was more than our profit margin. The bill for tickets for the Oberammergau 2010 Passion Play season increased by over £1 million, with a similar increase in the land costs of the Austrian part of the holiday. We did surcharge but decided that the amount of the increase was too large to pass on to our travellers. It is soul destroying to work hard, produce excellent holidays with great feed-back, but produce very little income.

Sadly, the cost of a typical Holy Land pilgrimage had doubled in the decade through factors outside of our control. The Middle East conflicts raised the price of oil, leading to higher air fares and currency exchange rates did the rest. In 2000, one British Pound was worth one Euro, 70 cents. Before the 2008 financial collapse, this had reduced to one Euro and 40 cents. The pound ended the decade just above parity, worth 40% less than its 2000 level.

This was a decade of challenges, which very few of our competitors managed to survive.

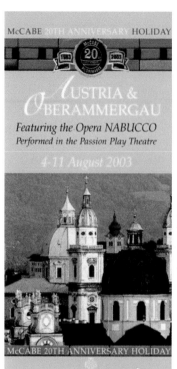

McCABE 20TH ANNIVERSARY HOLIDAY

*A*USTRIA &
*O*BERAMMERGAU

Featuring the Opera NABUCCO
Performed in the Passion Play Theatre

4-11 August 2003

McCABE 20TH ANNIVERSARY HOLIDAY

McCabe
PILGRIMAGES

McCabe Pilgrimages

Britain's foremost religious tour operator

Programmes & Prices for 2010

OBERAMMERGAU
2010

Holidays including the Passion Play

McCabe Pilgrimages

Oberammergau 2010

The villagers voted in 2010 to change the performance times. The debate divided the village, with older residents voting for the status quo - but younger residents won the day by a narrow majority, and the performance moved from being an all-day event to the afternoon and evening. This meant that working villagers could attend to business in the morning and balance their participation in the play with family and work. Play Director, Christian Stuckl, campaigned strongly for the change, which would also enable the dramatic second half, now in darkness, to be transformed by stage lighting.

Our view was mixed. Dramatically, the change was a spectacular success, but the late finish made it difficult for some to find their guest houses, and there was no longer the opportunity to share the experience over a relaxed dinner. Guests arriving for the shorter one-night stay, now arrived in the morning of the performance, whereas in previous seasons they had arrived the day before. We decided that the pattern of preparatory meetings and services at the Ecumenical Centre wouldn't work with the new timings, and with some sadness, we discontinued the chaplaincy.

There were many changes in the ten years between Passion Play seasons. Werner and Sybille had both left Panorama Tours and, together with Erica formed I-WB, our travel partner for Oberammergau 2010. This would be my third Oberammergau season partnered by Sybille. In the airline industry, there had been a major shake-up with low-cost carriers such as Ryanair and EasyJet becoming market leaders. For the first time, we decided not to charter our own aircraft, but to use only scheduled flights and to expand the number of departure airports to include Scotland.

Pictured above with Frederik Mayet and Andreas Richter who shared the role of Jesus. We shared an office with Andreas's sister, Gabby, who we liked to call Jesus's sister!

In the London office, Matthew worked with me in the two-year build-up to the season, then becoming an integral part of our team in Oberammergau village. Rachel took charge of our flight programme and we brought in four part-time staff. We expanded our office into the floor above, and we were ready to go again!

Icelandic Ash Cloud

The season started with bad portents: in March, Mount Eyjafjallajökull (spell-checked!) volcano in Iceland erupted for the first time in 200 years and eruptions continued intermittently for two months creating ash clouds in the atmosphere. The risk to aircraft was hard to determine so, as a precaution, on the worst affected days, flights were grounded. There were days with no flights at all in Europe. Our holidays to Oberammergau were a mix of people seeing the play at the beginning, middle or end of their holiday. Everybody did see the play, but those with the play at the beginning were most affected. Werner did a fantastic job at Munich airport managing flight delays and on occasions finding airport accommodation when flights were cancelled at short notice. Mercifully, the crisis only affected the first two weeks of the season.

After this experience, we decided to plan all future Oberammergau holidays with the play in the middle or end of the holiday, not the beginning. My favourite ash cloud story is an EL AL plane with our passengers returning from Israel being diverted in flight to Marseille in France. Andy had a friend in Marseille who met them on arrival and organised overnight accommodation. Werner negotiated with our Oberammergau coach partner, Albus, who had a coach within a hundred miles which diverted to meet the group. Apparently seamlessly, the group were met, overnighted, and escorted to Calais where our London office arranged a coach and escort to complete the group's journey. There are many similar stories which bring in to focus the ingenuity and camaraderie of the travel industry co-operating in a crisis, and the privilege it is to be a part of it.

We installed a first-class team in Oberammergau village to look after McCabe guests. Matthew was joined by Werner's daughter, Nicole and Angelica, a local. We shared an office in the village centre with Gabby Richter, whose brother was playing Jesus. My sister Anne took a turn helping in the village, as did Stuart, Emma, Rosemary, and others from the McCabe extended family including regular group leaders such as Bob Jackson. It remained a privilege to live and work in the village during the season.

Sadly, my mother Mollie died on 6 July. As fate would have it, we heard the news during a performance attended by family members including Andrew, my uncle, who'd travelled from India. It is times like these that you appreciate the support of the community. There was great co-operation to fill the gaps, as the funeral was arranged in Edinburgh, and attended by many of our team.

Our 2010 season of Austria and Oberammergau holidays was in many ways straightforward, after the freak ash cloud start to the season. We accommodated 12,000 travellers with few complaints, and a complex operation was handled professionally by a great team of staff in the UK, Austria and Germany. We were experts in our field, and did most things right, but the devaluation of the Pound in the 2008 Financial Crash meant that excellent holidays with great feed-back, once again produced very little tangible reward. There are few businesses like the travel industry which come with such responsibility, and where the rewards are so uncertain.

After Oberammergau, Matthew returned to Manchester where he met and married Joanna and is now developing a successful career in Public Relations. My retirement ambitions were again put on hold.

Oberammergau Passion Play 2010

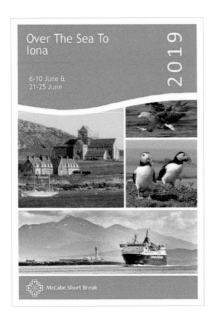

Over The Sea To
Iona

2019

6-10 June &
21-25 June

McCabe Short Break

ΙΗ ΒΑΙ ΦΟΡΟΣ

McCabe
PILGRIMAGES

Group Organisers Manual

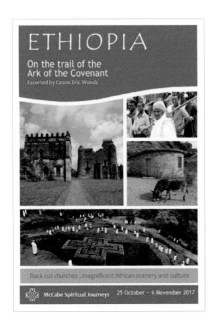

ETHIOPIA

On the trail of the
Ark of the Covenant
Escorted by Canon Eric Woods

Rock cut churches, magnificent African scenery and culture

McCabe Spiritual Journeys   25 October – 6 November 2017

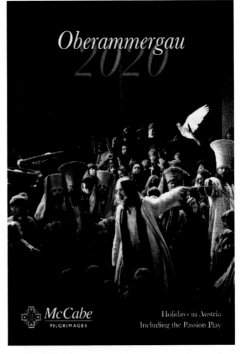

Oberammergau
2020

McCabe
PILGRIMAGES

Holidays in Austria
Including the Passion Play

A Decade of Calm

2011 - 2020

A Period of Relative Stability

For our fourth decade, with two major exceptions, we were blessed with political and financial stability. Staff numbers fluctuated at around eight. We sadly said good-bye to Letty and Nada, who both left the company on the births of their second children.

We welcomed Carol May, a member of our local church. Carol is an experienced Office Manager but arrived with no previous tour operating experience. Carol quickly learned how to use our reservations system and became a great asset with her empathy towards our clients, something that's difficult to teach.

Carol was joined by McCabe family friend Tim Lunn, a wizard with a spreadsheet and our financial statistics rose to new heights. Tim was also new to the world of tour operating but learned quickly and became a key member of our Oberammergau team.

I can't resist adding the picture below of Tim (in red) and his older brother Danny, taken in McCabe's first office. Danny, now a Graphic Designer, has also worked at McCabe from time to time.

Civil War in Syria

It was so sad to see Syria degenerate into civil war. We invested time and resources to introduce regular leaders to, what was for us, a new destination. An introductory tour of forty group organisers in 2011 led to twenty pilgrimages to Syria being arranged.

Visiting Syria took us back in time to a largely undeveloped, rural country where we drove through fields reminiscent of what the Holy Land once looked like. In Israel, we catch glimpses of the Biblical landscape, especially in Galilee, but the Israel of today is largely a modern, developed country. Crossing into the Hashemite Kingdom of Jordan, we step back in time to explore a country with wonderful desert vistas unchanged since the time of Moses - but driving through rural Syria was to step back even further and experience what the Middle East at the time of Jesus may have looked like. Few tourists visit Syria, especially the Christian sites, and we were made so welcome. A standout visit was to the convent of St Sergius at Maaloula, one of the oldest in Christendom pre-dating the Council of Nicaea (325AD), and to be welcomed by nuns, some of whom spoke Aramaic, the language of Jesus.

The uprising began while Rosemary was accompanying one of our parties in the country and, it's at times like these, that our membership of the Association of Independent Tour Operators comes into its own. We spoke to other companies working with Syria and, through AITO, were in daily contact with the British Foreign Office.

Syria is a good example of how McCabe responds to a political crisis. On the ground, Rosemary reported that our group was not experiencing any difficulty and the party were happy to continue, but the feedback we were receiving pointed to a rapidly deteriorating situation. We acted quickly and repatriated the party - before the Foreign Office made the same decision - and we cancelled upcoming departures.

The conflict in Syria escalated and ten years on, is not resolved: a tragedy for all concerned. Our experience was nothing compared to what happened to our partners in the country and the Syrian Christian community.

At Maaloula, the walls of the monastery remain intact, but sadly the interior was looted and mostly destroyed

For the company, this meant 2011 was another year with a financial deficit as we lost the promotional funds we had invested and the income from what would have been the successful launch of a new destination.

A Summer War in Gaza

The second political conflict to affect us began in the summer of 2014, when ongoing tension on the Gaza-Israel border erupted into full scale war. The conflict lasted fifty days and the statistics are horrendous. This was the largest loss of life in the region since the 1967 Six Day War. More than 6,000 rockets were fired, and in tightly packed Gaza, homes and infrastructure were destroyed on a huge scale. Lives lost numbered more than 2,000. A truce was agreed with both sides claiming victory.

An appeal from The McCabe Educational Trust raised £60,000 to help the Anglican run Al Ahli hospital in Gaza which was trying to cope with an unprecedented number of the severely injured. Israel is a small country, roughly the size of Wales but even so, normal life in Tel Aviv and Jerusalem continued throughout the conflict. We cancelled two summer pilgrimages but, after the ceasefire, our autumn groups all travelled. This was a rare case of a major Middle East conflagration that was not a financial disaster for us.

Planning For The Future

McCabe Pilgrimages has always had a natural business cycle, based on building the company up for an Oberammergau season every ten years, then reducing again afterwards, a balancing act which is not so easy to get right. As has been seen in our story so far, we are particularly vulnerable to events in the Middle East. Add to these, the vagaries of the exchange rate and other economic factors and future planning is always a bit of a guessing game.

After Oberammergau 2010, we focussed on a succession plan and for the first time brought in professional travel consultants to advise us. We commissioned management consultant, Richard Atkinson to analyse our strengths and weaknesses and give advice on a future strategy. Stewart Lambert, an expert in travel company sales, was asked to put a value on the business and we discussed the optimum time to sell. The third expert we brought on board was Richard Bass, a retired travel company owner who had successfully sold his own company some years before. Richard became a non-executive director for six months and set the agenda at a series of six board meetings, forcing us to take time out from the day-to-day running of the company and focus on the bigger picture. We took advice on board, and made some difficult decisions losing Katarina and Alison, two valuable staff members that, post Oberammergau, we couldn't justify keeping, and we reduced the physical size of our office, halving the rent.

The company was recognised by these experts as generally being in a good place, experiencing natural growth principally through word of mouth and, most importantly, we were offering a consistently good product which compared favourably with our competitors. Our principal challenge was that our core traveller base was getting older and smaller, mirroring the general decline in church attendance. If we didn't respond, it was likely that we would go into reverse gear and find ourselves managing the gradual decline of the company.

We looked at various options. One was to sell to a competitor and pass the challenge on to them. Selling a company like McCabe Pilgrimages is not straightforward as the risk to reward ratio is so uncertain with much of the business vulnerable to political unrest. Stewart Lambert prepared a proposal for us, and we decided to put the sale option on the shelf and re-visit it before the next Oberammergau season when the potential Oberammergau bonus would add to the company value and mitigate the Middle East risk factor.

It would also be important to demonstrate to any buyer that the company was not overly dependent on me, so we needed to think about appointing a new managing director. It was also clear that we were not making good use of our database. Mine and Rosemary's limited computer expertise and lack of marketing skills had to be addressed. Another urgent need was to introduce some new types of holidays to offset the decline in our traditional pilgrimages, but without losing focus on our core parish parties which paid the bills.

Embracing Change

The bedrock of McCabe is the parish pilgrimage. Alongside these parish groups, we look after larger pilgrimages, which typically number between fifty and a hundred travellers, and sometimes more. Examples include diocesan parties from St Albans and Southwark and the New Wine Church in South London. These present different challenges, with multiple coaches travelling together. A statistic I find interesting is that if you divide the total number of travellers in a year by the number of groups, the answer is always about 23. We pride ourselves on giving the same attention to a party of sixteen as to a party of fifty.

Word-of-mouth has been our principal source of growth, and very few church parties travel only once. Over the years, this steadily increasing and loyal base has enabled us to bounce back from crises on which many of our competitors have foundered.

The company took on board changes recommended by our management consultants. We introduced new destinations and, for the first time, offered these directly to our mailing list which we overhauled and now add to monthly. The challenge was to balance our politically vulnerable Holy Land trips with those to other destinations such as our journeys in the footsteps of St Paul through Greece and Turkey, and itineraries in Italy, Georgia, and Armenia, and recent additions Romania and Ethiopia. More below, but the most significant new initiatives were our sponsored walks and UK short break holidays.

A particular challenge identified was the ageing church population and in parallel, the increasing average age of a McCabe traveller. With church membership getting older and in decline, an enthusiastic pilgrimage organiser often has quite a small number of suitable candidates to invite on pilgrimage. The rising cost of a pilgrimage has also become a limiting factor. I think the pattern of McCabe Holy Land pilgrimages may change in the coming years, with fewer individual parish groups, and more of the larger diocesan pilgrimages drawing from many parishes. Working with the mega, mostly black, charismatic churches like New Wine, has been an exciting challenge, but McCabe has shown that it can find a meeting of minds with churches, until now, outside of our experience and comfort zone.

We also see a trend of individuals joining tours which have no association with their local church. Perhaps this will open the door to more ecumenical pilgrimages, which were the passion of Arthur Payton at Inter Church Travel. During the next ten years, we may see McCabe evolving away from parish groups to individuals joining larger pilgrimages with a particular theme or celebrity leadership.

We have missed Robert Trimble, who was instrumental in our early years building relationships with church leaders. When Robert left, we never really replaced him and, with this in mind, we looked to recruit a church 'insider' when thinking about the succession and life at McCabe after my retirement.

A Decade of Sponsored Walks

This was the decade of the McCabe Educational Trust sponsored walk. Four were organised, raising £200,000 for partner projects in the Holy Land.

The initiative came from Revd Elizabeth Price, a McCabe pilgrim from Chingford who, on 2 January 2011, walked around the Old City walls of Jerusalem raising awareness and funds for three special people, Alice Sahhar, and her daughters Najwa and Samar, the 'trinity' behind the boys' and girls' homes in Bethany. Alice was the entrepreneur, opening Jeel al Amal in 1972. Sadly, Alice died in 2008, but her daughters continue the work.

Elizabeth presented the McCabe Educational Trust with a cheque for £1,000 and an idea was born. With Elizabeth's co-operation, MET developed the idea of the 'Trinity Sponsored Walk' and increased the scale with around eighty participants on the four walks that were to follow.

2012 Our First Walk

The first MET walk in January 2012 had eighty participants including Elizabeth, McCabe Pilgrimages staff, MET trustees, loyal supporters, and friends from the Jerusalem area. We dedicated the event to the memory of Alice. On a cold, rainy day, we walked three times around the Old City walls and raised £65,000 for a 'trinity' of Christian-led projects: Jeel al Amal Boys' Home in Bethany and, in Bethlehem, the Al Shurooq Blind School and The Rehabilitation Centre.

The event was part of a memorable week in the Holy Land with an emphasis on getting to know the people that the McCabe Educational Trust supports. Visits to pilgrim sites were secondary to the unique experience of meeting the boys at Jeel and listening to the concerns of Najwa and her staff.

We were exposed to the difficulties experienced daily by this small Christian community doing such remarkable work in a politically and economically hostile environment. Our visits to the projects were humbling and re-affirmative, bringing home that this is the essence of a McCabe Holy Land pilgrimage. Evenings were enhanced by guests from the projects joining us and sharing the challenges of their everyday lives.

This event, and the three that were to follow, were opportunities for MET supporters to meet each other and the McCabe staff and were an expression of the shared experience that brings McCabe travellers back on repeated pilgrimages.

2014 Our Second Walk

Celebrating Thirty Years of Pilgrimage

We celebrated the 30th anniversary of McCabe in 2014 with our second Sponsored Walk. We gathered on the Mount of Olives and followed the Palm Sunday route into the Old City of Jerusalem, following the Via Dolorosa to the Holy Sepulchre. After a lunch break, the party divided, with some completing the day walking back to the hotel on top of the Old City walls.

Visits to MET projects remained central to our week, but additional highlights were two gala dinners hosted by the Golden Walls and Ron Beach hotels. Our project and business partners, guides and their families joined us to celebrate thirty years of McCabe pilgrimage. For our guides (pictured below) the evening at the Golden Walls Hotel was extra special, as the nature of their job means that they are seldom all together in one room. These evenings were inspirational, showing us the esteem in which McCabe is held.

Nada designed a different T shirt for each walk, and some participants have all four. We presented Fahmi at the Golden Walls and the Amsalem brothers at the Ron Beach with a plate commemorating our thirty year partnership with their hotels. Our Sponsored Walk weeks were a balance of fundraising, fellowship, and worship. Above, two MET Trustees, Brian Leathard and Kevin Dunne celebrate the Eucharist in a cave in the Bethlehem Shepherds Fields.

2016 Our Third Walk

For our third walk in 2016, our party of ninety participants stayed in Bethlehem. We had a very special welcome from the Mayor who joined us for dinner on our first evening and spoke to us about the challenges of living in Bethlehem today.

During our four days in the birthplace of Jesus we divided into smaller groups. Particularly memorable was a visit to Aida refugee camp where some of our party spent the morning cooking with Palestinian women. Our friends at Al Shurooq and the Rehabilitation Centre appreciated us staying in the town, as they were able to join us for meals and other activities. For the second half of the week, we stayed in Tiberias.

Our walk this time was to be in two parts: part one had a desert theme, walking in the Bethlehem area to Mar Saba monastery. We then completed our challenge with a glorious walk along the shore of the Sea of Galilee. We finished our pilgrimage with worship, sailing across the Sea of Galilee.

2018 Our Fourth Walk

We are indebted to MET vice chair, The Very Revd Geoffrey Marshall for researching and developing our walking routes. For our fourth walk in 2018, Geoffrey came up with the idea of three shorter walks. We began in Jerusalem, walking along the Via Dolorosa, then, in the Judean desert, we walked in Wadi Qelt to St George's Monastery. The culmination of our week was a walk in the Huleh Valley of Upper Galilee, a magnet for migratory birds.

To the sound of birdsong, we walked around Argamon Lake. Our drivers had great fun driving golf carts and assisting the less able walkers. As always, we visited MET projects and shared time with the wonderful people who run them.

The operating costs of these experiences were donated by McCabe Pilgrimages, and our partners in the Holy Land reduced their prices so that the walks were accessible to a wide range of participants.

From a company point of view, these pilgrimages strengthened our sense of purpose, and highlighted to McCabe staff both in Jerusalem and the UK that an essential part of any McCabe pilgrimage is meeting and supporting fellow Christians in whichever destination we are travelling to.

Short Break Holidays Introduced in 2015

As part of our management consultancy process, we participated in an AITO led survey of our travellers. The most interesting discovery was that a significant number of McCabe travellers go on holiday three or four times a year, with many of these holidays being short breaks in the UK - and there was a desire to travel more frequently with McCabe.

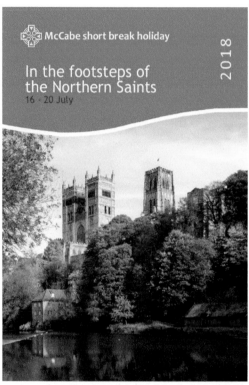

We responded by offering our first Short Break holiday in 2015. The programme was developed by Revd Kevin Dunne, MET trustee and loyal McCabe leader. The four-day programme 'In Search of the Northern Saints' was based in Durham University accommodation and included walking at low tide to the Holy Island of Lindisfarne. We initially offered thirty places, but this grew to three consecutive weekends with 150 participants. This became an annual event, each year making changes to keep the itinerary fresh. For instance, one year we added Hadrian's Wall, and another year a ride on the Yorkshire Steam Railway, but we always kept to the 'Northern Saints' theme.

A natural progression was a short break programme to the Scottish Holy Island of Iona, which we had last visited in the 1980s when Moses Donaldson was minister on the neighbouring island of Mull. Iona is a jewel of an island but has very limited accommodation, so we based our group in the Isle of Mull Hotel and made day trips to Iona and Staffa. The highlight was worship in Iona Abbey, redolent with memories of the Macleod family's role in the 1940s reconstruction – and Ursula Macleod's role in founding McCabe Travel. Revd Iain Paton, MET trustee, pioneered this trip and the following year researched and conducted a follow-up itinerary based in Edinburgh University accommodation and visiting the border abbeys of Scotland.

In 2018, extending the idea to foreign holidays, seventy McCabe travellers were part of a memorable weekend in Oberammergau participating in the ceremony announcing the cast for the 2010 Passion Play. Our guide was 'Mary Magdalene'. The weekend was planned as a staff training exercise for the Passion Play season, now only two years away, and marked the launch of Oberammergau sales.

Geoffrey Marshall (pictured here with his group at Finisterre) had developed our sponsored walk itineraries and he now took the concept further, pioneering our first one week walking tour along the final hundred miles of the Camino to Santiago de Compostela. Our previous Camino tours had all been a mixture of walking and coaching. Another success! The series of trips that followed included one in partnership with London's Christian radio station, Premier Radio.

Short break holidays are now the main feature of a McCabe summer and, like our sponsored walks, are an opportunity for regular travellers to meet and travel together on shorter, less expensive holidays. We also use them as an opportunity for our normally office-based staff to meet our travellers and McCabe staff accompany each trip. Many clients now travel on two and sometimes three McCabe holidays each year. From a business point of view these summer holidays fill a gap in our pilgrimage year when it is too hot for travel to the Holy Land.

On Pilgrimage with New Wine Church

The most fun I ever had on a pilgrimage was when Andy and I escorted a party from New Wine Church on their first Holy Land pilgrimage. Preparing for the trip, I attended worship in their transformed cinema building in Woolwich, and was bowled over by the music, the enthusiasm, and the welcome I received in this predominantly black, charismatic fellowship.

We realised early on that this pilgrimage would be very different. New Wine is a church centred on prayer and praise. At a preparatory meeting we began with a prayer session lasting twenty minutes with everybody joining in. This would become the pattern on the pilgrimage.

Where normally, we would include four visits in a morning, we now planned a programme with no more than two. Our guides would talk very little, as the leadership at each site we visited conducted ex tempore worship of indeterminate length. This was a breath of fresh air for us and we learned so much from New Wine's completely different approach to pilgrimage.

At the Jordan River, the party of seventy all donned white robes and were baptised by full immersion in a ceremony lasting more than two hours. There was laughter as women bound their heads in cling film to protect their hair.

We enjoyed continuous singing from the choir and smiles all round as the two pastors, waist deep in the river, baptised their flock with a mixture of humour and reverence.

They so enjoyed being in the Holy Land and their faith was infectious with guides, drivers and onlookers drawn in. At the Basilica of St Anne beside the Pool of Bethesda, there is an understanding that parties do not stay too long to allow other groups time there as well. The acoustics here are wonderful, and other parties joined in as the New Wine choir sang and prayed for almost an hour.

Logistically, it was a challenge and our planned programme, including lunch slots, changed by the hour – all possible with mobile phones.

A typical pilgrimage day started at 5 am with an hour of prayer in the meeting room. (Andy or I were there earlier each morning to make sure the door was not locked and to turn the lights on.) We were on the road by 8 and usually back later than the planned 5 pm. An evening meeting of praise completed the day. We and they slept well!

Supporters Tours to Dr Graham's Homes in India

My sister and I were born in Kalimpong, where our parents served as missionaries at Dr Graham's Homes. When my mother died, I accepted an invitation to join the UK Fundraising Committee and continue the family tradition.

A highpoint was escorting two McCabe trips to the Homes with the twin objectives of existing benefactors meeting the children they were supporting, and hopefully we would inspire new sponsors. In 2015, our party of thirty was a wonderful mix of people including many with connections to the school and newcomers inspired by its story.

Leadership was shared with Margaretta Purtill, who had attended the school when I was a child, McCabe director Stuart Lynch, and my sister Anne Pears, who was our nurse and kept busy with the usual stomach upsets to the more serious altitude sickness of one of our party.

We were delighted to have Sheena Parrott on board, a family friend whose father had been principal in the 1950s, and Chris Christenson, another family friend, and professional photographer responsible for all the good pictures in our brochures, and none of the bad!

In Kolkata, we were joined by Bradley Mawer and his wife Shweta, former Homes' Head Boy, and Head Girl. Bradley had once been a sponsored child and both were wonderful ambassadors for the school they loved.

This was a holiday in the same mould as our first ever McCabe journey to India 32 years earlier, with an emphasis on meeting the people, past and present, who had played a part in this wonderful institution. In Kolkata, past principal Bernard Brookes, spoke eloquently and introduced us to three favourite former pupils, one of whom was Margaretta. We had receptions with recent school leavers and with board members – the perfect introduction to our visit to Kalimpong.

The twin towns of Kalimpong and Darjeeling are not easily accessible and for our week in the hills, we travelled in a convoy of quite luxurious jeeps with Nepalese drivers. We visited a tea plantation and a Buddhist monastery, rode on the Toy Train, and got up early to watch the sun rise over the Himalayan peaks – awe inspiring - but the highlight was our three-day visit to the school.

The Homes do not disappoint, and our visit was made special by the staff, past and present, who participated in our programme, and the children that we spent time with. The trip achieved its purpose with seven new sponsors coming forward and the McCabe Educational Trust taking on sponsorship of five children. We repeated this trip two years later, with many of the party, including Margaretta, Bradley and Shweta who again shared the leadership, returning for a second visit.

Travelling with a large party in a remote area has its challenges and often we had to think on our feet. Arriving in Kalimpong at the Silver Oaks Hotel, I let my guard down as we were well received at a lovely property. I invited the party to meet in the bar for pre-dinner drinks and a briefing on the following day's school visit. I came down twenty minutes before the meeting to discover one barman, with very little in the way of drinks. We hastily sent someone to the market to buy whatever was available and, for our time at the Silver Oaks, I got the co-operation of the hotel to serve our own drinks. The party were happy that drinks were now compliments of McCabe and accepted the lack of variety with good humour. At dinner, volunteers from the party had fun acting as waiters, and we served our own wine.

This is our India party with, kneeling in the foreground, Chris Christenson a professional photographer and friend who has travelled on many trips giving us great images for our brochures.

Retirement

and New Beginnings

McCabe Overseas Partners

A pilgrimage is a joint venture arranged by McCabe in London and carefully selected representatives overseas. We look for partners who share our values and, more straightforwardly, people that we get on with. Finding the right match is not easy and sometimes 'you have to kiss a lot of frogs to find your prince - or princess!' After a few false starts, we found the right match in Israel and Palestine, Jordan, Egypt, Turkey, India and Nepal, Greece, Italy, Spain, Austria and Oberammergau, and these people have become part of the fabric of my life and of the company's.

With my retirement imminent, a big reason not to sell the company to an outsider was to protect this McCabe network. Any competitor buying McCabe would be likely to disband our team in favour of their own.

In Jerusalem, McCabe has two second homes with the Albina and Nashashibi families. In both cases, our relationship has lasted more than thirty years and we now work with the next generation.

We began our partnership with Francois Albina, who sadly passed on at an early age, as tragically did his son, Tony. Vehanoush joined the business and took on the reins, and today her daughter Natasha is following the family tradition as our partner in Jerusalem. Walid Nabber, pictured on the right, provides continuity having worked in the Albina office since the time of Francois. The Albina family are McCabe in the Holy Land and integral to all we do, supervising the day to day running of our Holy Land pilgrimages.

Fahmi Nashashibi is a similar age to me and back at the beginning of our relationship took over the running of the family hotel from his father Rashid and mother Widad (pictured here). Fahmi married Marlene, who at the time was employed in the Albina office. Much later, their daughter, Nada (pictured here) would become a key employee in the McCabe London office. Fahmi has increased the size of his hotel, renovated it beyond recognition and changed the name from the old-fashioned 'Pilgrims Palace' to the Golden Walls, where today most McCabe pilgrims are accommodated.

In Tiberias, the three brothers Aaron, Mula and Avram Amsalem could not be more loyal and supportive. When I arrived in Tiberias in 1976, the Ron Beach was a restaurant, but under Aaron's supervision, a hotel was created, and gradually expanded from one floor to two to now three, with 160 beds. The brothers live up to my father's motto 'Work hard, think big, and never lose the common touch'. Each brother has a role to play. Aaron is the architect, Avram looks after reservations and Mula is food and beverage. Together, they have achieved remarkable growth without losing their very real personal connection with business partners like us, and their pilgrim guests. We have grown up together and we couldn't wish for a more secure McCabe base in the Galilee.

The Nazareth Coach Company has grown from a few coaches in 1976 to today being one of Israel's largest. Business lunches with the Afifi family are always memorable. I particularly like the fact that lunch for six would often grow to lunch for twelve as drivers and office staff would join us, reflecting the respect permeating the company with Managing Director and driver comfortable lunching together.

Our relationship was strengthened when Letty, the daughter-in-law of one of the owners, joined our London office.

Across the Jordan River, Ghada Najjar worked for two Jordanian travel companies and also lived and worked for a time in Greece. Again, for more than thirty years, she has been our partner and the McCabe relationship moved with her every time she moved office – including to Greece. When she started her own business, we were her first client. Karma House is now one of the largest travel companies in Jordan.

Jordan has changed beyond recognition but it remains a particularly friendly destination and we have had great fun together with Ghada chartering steam trains, organising camping in Wadi Rum and arranging meals in Crusader castles.

Yasser Zeid is our partner in Egypt and he would co-ordinate with Ghada in an innovative McCabe holiday combining Jordan with the Sinai peninsula, when we would charter a yacht to sail between the two countries. I feel sorry for Yasser, a man full of ideas, but very many of our pilgrimages were cancelled because of political unrest. Lots of work for no tangible result.

In Turkey, Bikem Ronay and Seniz have also been with us since the beginning and together we developed itineraries throughout Turkey, featuring St Paul's journeys, the Seven Churches of Revelation and the earliest days of the Christian church, making Turkey our second most popular destination. They made our job easy, working with this vast country which they knew intimately whether we were staying in Istanbul, Ephesus or remote Cappadocia.

Prem Rana is another friend whose career has paralleled McCabe's. Our first pilgrimage in 1984 was looked after by Prem when he worked with Nepal's only international travel company, Yeti. In those days, communication with remote Nepal was so bad, a Yeti representative would meet every incoming flight and the party leader would hand over a letter with instructions for their stay. Yeti, often with no notice of a group's arrival, would make arrangements on the spot!

Prem and Purnima started their own business and we were their first clients. Today the business has grown and includes the Summerhill Guest House in Kathmandu and the luxury Begnas resort near Pokhara, both used by McCabe travellers. Prem also opened an office in India and now also looks after our Kalimpong adventures. Prem and Purnima have become close friends and a McCabe delegation were very privileged to attend their daughter Priyanka's wedding in Kathmandu.

Ghada was our partner in Greece while she had her 'Sabbatical' years there, but when she returned to Jordan, she introduced us to Steve Vasiliades, who quickly understood what we were looking for. We thank Steve for introducing us to a modern convent situated very close to the historic Meteora monasteries. Visiting and contrasting the modern and ancient communities became the highlight of a McCabe Greek itinerary.

For McCabe, Spain is the Camino to Santiago de Compostela. We were introduced to Andres Lopez who, with a Spanish father and German mother, brought efficiency and a great love for Spain. Our take on the Camino, developed with Andres, was to coach the five hundred miles of *The Way* through Spain, visiting historic sites and churches and each day walking an interesting section of the route. Later, with Andres' help we would offer the first McCabe completely walking holidays as part of our Short Breaks programme.

Salzburg has become my second home and my favourite city. Sybille married Richard, a chef, and together they run the first class Brunnauer Restaurant, but she is still part of the team offering advice and keeping us on the right lines. Werner Bischof is also retired, but likewise with McCabe's fourth Oberammergau on the horizon is ready to give advice.

It is humbling to add up the number of people who co-operate on a typical pilgrimage, and very sobering to consider the impact on them when a tour is cancelled, or a season of tours, or, as has happened, years without travellers. Perhaps the biggest reward from being a Tour Operator is being treated as a family member in so many countries. This is not something you can buy at any price.

Oberammergau 2020 moved to 2022

I always say that every Oberammergau is different from the last, and this one has been no exception. The Covid pandemic struck just before the beginning of the season and, what promised to be one of our most successful years financially, turned out to be the opposite.

We promptly offered our travellers a full refund, or the option of postponing to new 2022 dates. About half retained their booking for the future date, and we are grateful for this support.

There are so many unknowns about travel after this pandemic that planning for 2022 is a bit like looking into a crystal ball. We wonder which airlines will still be flying and on which routes and at what fares, and which hotels will be able to offer the same level of service, and whether it will be at a price we can afford. The actual Oberammergau season lasts only twenty weeks. We started planning for this one in 2017 so, by the time of the first performance, five years' work will have gone into the project. Much of this work has been like 'Groundhog Day'. In March 2020, all preparations were ready but, during the last year, we have had to cancel and rebook travellers and re-contract all our hotels and air seats.

Effect of the 2020 / 2021 Pandemic

The pandemic struck in March 2020, ten weeks before the first performance of the Oberammergau Passion Play. Three years of planning and investment were about to come together in what would be McCabe's fourth Oberammergau season, and my final challenge before retirement.

The first months were full of uncertainty as we didn't know then how serious the situation would become. The initial feeling was that perhaps some early performances would be cancelled, and we tried to protect dates later in the season for our early groups, well aware that the Passion Play is only performed every ten years, and we didn't want anyone to miss out. With our Holy Land parties, we cancelled March, then April but fully expected our May groups to travel. We were very busy re-arranging these early pilgrimages for the following year, which wasn't so easy as hotels were already fully booked for the following year's peak dates. This became the pattern for the rest of the year. We were very busy – but working hard with no income.

We entered the pandemic in a stronger position than many companies, with a positive balance sheet and no debts. We also had a full order book and were comfortable with staff numbers, the size of our office space and general running costs. All in all, we had a tight ship. As the crisis lengthened, we made plans for short, medium, and long-term scenarios. We took advantage of government help in the form of a business interruption loan, rates relief and the furlough scheme.

We cancelled or postponed tours and offered travellers an immediate refund or the option of transferring to a future holiday. A big factor that fell in our favour was the decision of Oberammergau village to postpone the event by two years and not one. This gave us time to regroup and plan for the new season. Our biggest risk factor bizarrely was the crisis finishing quickly. In this case we may not have received refunds for a very large number of Oberammergau flights already fully paid for.

As the crisis stretches into a second year, the challenges facing all travel companies are evolving. It is not at all clear which companies will survive or how those that do, will change the way they work to meet new challenges. For instance, we expect fewer flights and higher air fares; some hotels and restaurants may not re-open; in the UK, we may bring Covid under control, but the worldwide situation could remain uncertain for much longer.

At McCabe, we are fortunate to have longstanding partners and we share a confidence that together we will go forwards strongly after this experience. We have plans in place to keep the office structure fully functioning even if there is no travel in 2021. The cost of doing this is large, but we have decided to invest in the future. Every ten years, Oberammergau is a significant marker in the history of the company. The fact that the pandemic coincided with an Oberammergau year meant a big loss of income, but also gives us a firm basis for survival as many of our travellers rebooked for the 2022 season. This, together with so many re-arranged Holy Land pilgrimages, gives us every confidence that we will bounce back strongly after the pandemic.

The McCabe Educational Trust also lost much of its regular income. To counter this, trustees launched an appeal at Easter 2020 specifically for the Bethlehem Rehabilitation Centre, on the front-line coping with the pandemic sweeping through Bethlehem.

We were able to send them £50,000. At Christmas, when it was becoming clear the crisis would be ongoing, we asked for help to support our key projects through the coming year. We are grateful for the wonderful response, with an additional £100,000 donated by loyal McCabe supporters. With these extra funds we expect to increase our grant giving in 2021, when our supported projects will need our help more than ever.

We won't receive any income from Oberammergau until after a successful series of holidays in 2022, demonstrating again the precarious nature of the travel industry, where much work, investment and energy can be expended with no guarantee of any reward.

McCabe Pilgrimages Under New Ownership

I had tried to leave McCabe Pilgrimages at what in hindsight was the peak of the company - our bumper Millennium year. Middle East politics intervened, and I stayed on for another twenty years and I have no regrets about that decision. But now, at 67 years old, I knew this really was the time to retire, and plans for the succession were well advanced before the pandemic struck.

Few family firms these days are passed from father to son or daughter. This is a trend that I have followed over the years and discussed with partners worldwide. Education is to blame, and it was our choice to educate our children! Angus and Eva have been introduced to a world of opportunities and they have always been encouraged to find their own direction. They have also witnessed the long hours, stress, and uncertain rewards of their father's career. But what a privilege for them to grow up in the McCabe Pilgrimages' environment, travelling widely from a very young age and being exposed to so many different cultures, which are now part of who they are and will be. I remember the two of them, five or six years old, in the Sinai desert happily playing with a Bedouin girl of similar age on a rockslide as Lynne and I sat cross-legged on the sand, coffee on the fire and camels around, discussing Project Sinai plans with her father.

Back in 2011 we began discussing the possible sale of the company with management consultant Stewart Lambert. We returned to this conversation in 2018, when a decision was made not to sell the company to an outsider, but instead to pursue a management buyout. I was happy to relinquish my shareholding in favour of Rosemary and Stuart, who would continue as share-holding directors, and a new MD also with a shareholding would be appointed.

We were fortunate to be introduced to Paul Ellerby (pictured here with Natasha on the Sea of Galilee), the essential new piece in the McCabe jigsaw.

Paul wasn't looking for a new job when our head-hunters persuaded him to speak to us. Paul uses a word from my childhood and feels 'called' to the position of McCabe Managing Director. In Paul, we have a combination of skills that our recruitment experts advised we were unlikely to find. Paul is a marketing expert with excellent computer skills and has a varied career in travel management behind him. Paul is also a committed Christian, a leader in his local church and studying to be ordained into the Anglican ministry, where he intends to minister on a non-stipendiary basis alongside his Directorship of McCabe.

When the pandemic struck in March 2020, the management buyout had been agreed and initialled. The cancellation of the rest of the year's business and the postponement of the Oberammergau season changed everything and unsurprisingly, the new team decided that now was not the right time to take over a travel company.

For the next few months our focus was on the crisis at hand and Paul, Rosemary and I made the urgent decisions necessary for survival.

In the summer, Stewart Lambert put a new proposal on the table. This was based on the original plan, but with an additional element. Stewart was part of Firebird, a new consortium of travel experts with a programme offering help to small travel businesses trying to cope with the pandemic. Stewart knew McCabe well and believed Firebird could add an extra dimension to put the management buyout back on the table. Importantly, Paul and Rosemary agreed.

I had decided to retire regardless of a deal and was delighted that a way forward had been found which kept staff in place and with the promise that the company would continue with the same ethos. The changeover was completed at Christmas 2020 and Lynne and I retired. Stuart Lynch also stepped down from his McCabe directorship.

Paul became Managing Director, Rosemary Company Secretary and, representing the Firebird Partnership, Ian Finlay joined the Board. Rachel, Carol, and Tim are the key continuing staff as we wait for travel to return after the pandemic. I am confident that the new team has the expertise required to meet the opportunities of the coming years.

The McCabe Educational Trust, as an independent charity is unaffected by the changeover, but Paul and Rosemary are committed to keeping the Trust an integral part of the McCabe Pilgrimages' offering. Stuart Lynch remains a Trust director and Lynne and I will become Trust administrators. We look forward to the pandemic receding when one of our first planned events will be the fifth MET Sponsored Walk.

All crises come to an end, and I expect McCabe under new ownership but with the continuity of excellent staff, to be fit and ready for 2022 which, with the postponed Oberammergau season, as well as many re-arranged pilgrimages offers the prospect of a speedy return to business as usual. Like so many times before, McCabe will bounce back, but there is no doubt that this has been the most expensive set back in the history of the company and, if it had happened when we were younger, we would have struggled to survive.

With minimal notice, our income reduced to zero with no timeframe of how long the crisis would last. This is also the case for our partners: coaches, guides, restaurants, hotels, and airlines. We had been prudent in the preceding years to build up the capital base of the company and this, together with a government backed loan and other help, including furloughed salaries, has enabled staff to be kept on board and the office open.

It is remarkable that the management changeover enabling my retirement was agreed in such a difficult context. I have mixed feelings about leaving the company I formed 37 years ago, but the time is right for me, and right for the company. New ideas and new thinking are required to take McCabe Pilgrimages forward in a rapidly changing environment.

Postscript

In the autumn of 1992 on a group tour of India with Moses Donaldson, we were visiting the Taj Mahal and a local photographer pestered us to have our photograph taken on the then famous bench where Princess Diana had posed alone a few months earlier to demonstrate her loneliness in an unhappy marriage. My thoughts were on the party which we were in charge of and I said no. Moses over-ruled my objection saying that the moment will not come again and the party will be fine for five minutes without us.

I admire the people I have shared my life with who have learned the art of living in the moment. Tomorrow may not always be there, and today will soon be gone.